T0319587

YING WANG
CHIA-HUEI WU

WORK AND
PERSONALITY CHANGE

What We Do Makes Who We Are

BRISTOL
UNIVERSITY
PRESS

First published in Great Britain in 2021 by

Bristol University Press
University of Bristol
1-9 Old Park Hill
Bristol
BS2 8BB
UK
t: +44 (0)117 954 5940
e: bup-info@bristol.ac.uk

Details of international sales and distribution partners are available at bristoluniversitypress.co.uk

British Library Cataloguing in Publication Data
A catalogue record for this book is available from the British Library

ISBN 978-1-5292-0755-2 hardcover
ISBN 978-1-5292-0758-3 ePub
ISBN 978-1-5292-0757-6 ePdf

Contents

Figures

Notes on Authors

Ying Wang is Senior Lecturer in Management at RMIT University, Australia. Her research interests include personality and individual differences, positive organisational behaviour and diversity management. Her work has been published in internationally leading academic journals such as the *Journal of Applied Psychology* and the *Annual Review of Organizational Psychology and Organizational Behavior*, and she was a past editor of the book series *Advances in Global Leadership*. Beyond academia, Lena worked for a decade as a practitioner specialising in personality testing, personnel selection and leadership development. She received her PhD from the University of Sheffield, UK.

Chia-Huei Wu is Professor in Organisational Psychology at the University of Leeds, UK. His research in organisational behaviour focuses on proactive behaviour, personality development, work design and employees' subjective well-being. His work has appeared in internationally leading academic journals, including *Academy of Management Journal*, the *Journal of Applied Psychology* and the *Journal of Management,* among others. He is the author of the book *Employee Proactivity in Organizations: An Attachment Perspective*. Before joining Leeds, Chia-Huei was Associate Professor at Durham University (2018–2020), and Assistant Professor at London School of Economics (2013–2018). He is a current associate editor for the *Journal of Management*. He received his PhD from the University of Western Australia.

Preface

Who are we? Are we 'set in stone' since adulthood or can we be malleable in who we are? Setting out to explore these questions in a work and vocational context, we hope to contribute to an increasingly recognised, dynamic perspective on human personality.

We are grateful for those scholars in personality psychology and organisational psychology who have inspired our interest in this topic. We also thank those individuals in our lives who either provide living examples of personality change or who have helped us to become better versions of ourselves.

This book is dedicated to academics, practitioners and students who study personality and its implication in the workplace. It is also dedicated to all individuals who are curious about how their personality can be changed by their environment, and those who make brave and persistent efforts in changing themselves.

ONE

What Personality Is and Why It Matters for Organisations

As individuals we all have unique characteristics that make us different from one another, and personality forms one of these important characteristics. Because of our personality differences, we tend to have different ways of thinking, feeling, behaving and relating to others and approaching the world. More importantly, personality has important implications in our lives – it impacts our social and interpersonal relationships, academic and work performance, mental health and well-being and even our physical health and longevity.

However, this is not to say that we should adopt a deterministic perspective about personality or a pessimistic belief that our lives will turn out in certain ways because of how our personality is engineered. As we will describe later, despite having relative stability, personality is not fixed, and instead can be changed by a vast range of life events and experiences. The authors' particular interest rests on how such change occurs in the work and vocational domain – a domain that is of critical importance to us due to the substantial amount of time we spend in this domain during our lives. By drawing on a wealth of the latest research evidence in personality psychology and organisational psychology, we intend to present how and why such change can happen and what we can do to facilitate this change in a positive and meaningful way.

This first chapter is a foundational chapter in which we provide a brief review of how personality is conceptualised, as well as how personality has been studied (and the results of those studies applied) in the work context. This chapter is intentionally kept very brief so that we can quickly move onto the change perspective of personality in the remaining chapters.

What is personality?

Personality as a concept has attracted broad interest for thousands of years. As early as the fourth century BC, Greek physicians proposed four temperamental types that differentiate individuals from one another – the sanguine, choleric, melancholic and phlegmatic – primarily based on individuals' bodily fluids (i.e. 'humours'). Since the development of psychology as a scientific discipline, personality has taken a central position in the discipline for the purpose of understanding individual differences, with numerous perspectives and discussions undertaken throughout the 20th century. Perspectives that originated from different schools of thought, for instance from biological (e.g. Buss, Eysenck), humanistic (e.g. Maslow, Rogers), psychodynamic (e.g. Freud, Jung), behavioural perspective (e.g. Skinner), cognitive (e.g. Mischel, Bandura) and trait (e.g. Allport, Cattell) approaches to individual differences, have each contributed their unique understanding and collectively informed the development of the study of personality as a field (see Cloninger, 2009, for a review).

Contemporary conceptualisations of personality tend to assume a holistic understanding of personality, seeing it as something that broadly represents individuality. Funder (1997, pp 1–2) defined personality as 'an individual's characteristic pattern of thought, emotion, and behaviour, together with the psychological mechanisms – hidden or not – behind these patterns'. Others follow similar approaches in defining personality as, for instance, 'relatively enduring patterns of thoughts, feelings, and behaviours that distinguish individuals from one another' (Roberts & Mroczek, 2008, p 31), or 'a spectrum of individual attributes that consistently distinguish people from one another in terms of their basic tendencies to think, feel, and act in certain ways' (Ones et al, 2005, p 390).

Although the trait-based approach has had a major influence on contemporary understanding of personality, many consider personality to encompass broader domains in the whole-person system, including, for instance, goals and motivations, self-esteem, values and needs, as well as personal schemas which describe how individuals make sense of the world and life narratives that describe people's sense-making of their life journey (e.g. Dunlop, 2015; Kandler et al, 2014; McAdams & Olson, 2010; McCrae & Costa, 2008; Roberts & Wood, 2006). In general, although the conceptualisation of personality can take on a somewhat different focus among different researchers, it is commonly agreed that personality acts as the bedrock of psychological individuality. It is necessary, however, to point out that given the trait-based approach has been mostly studied in the literature on personality at work and personality change over the last three decades, most evidence and discussions in this book are drawn from that perspective. Here we provide a brief review on this perspective.

The trait-based perspective of personality

The most well-known personality framework is 'the Big Five', which was established in early 1990s (Digman, 1990; Funder, 1994; Goldberg, 1990, 1993; McCrae & Costa, 2003). The Big Five was developed from a lexical approach based on years of review and compilation of personality-related adjectives from English dictionaries. Then, facilitated by the advancement of factor reduction techniques, researchers were able to identify common themes from a large volume of words so that high-order factors could be uncovered (Allport & Odbert, 1936; Cattell, 1943, 1945; Fiske, 1949; Galton, 1884; Norman, 1963; Tupes & Christal, 1992). These efforts have led to the conclusion that five high-order factors – identified as extraversion, agreeableness, openness to experience, conscientiousness and emotional stability (or its opposite form, neuroticism) – can describe all English words relating to individuals' personalities and are thus sufficiently broad and comprehensive to describe the personality domain. This personality framework emerged from the English language, but it was also replicated in other cultures (e.g. McCrae & Terracciano, 2005; McCrae & Costa, 1997).

The establishment of the Big Five is an important milestone in personality literature, as it brought a resurgence of wide interest and acceptance to the use of personality in predicting work behaviours and performance, a point that was criticised vehemently during the '60s (e.g. Guion & Gottier, 1965; Locke & Hulin, 1962; Michel, 1968), which silenced personality research for several decades. Hence, the Big Five is often mentioned as having brought about a renaissance in personality research (e.g. Barrick & Ryan, 2003; Kroeck & Brown, 2003; Viswesvaran & Ones, 2010), and such interest continues to this day.

Although the Big Five model has gained the most popularity, other personality frameworks have also been proposed. The Big Three, which consists of psychoticism, extraversion and neuroticism, was developed by the prominent psychologist Hans Eysenck, although this framework was used less in work settings (Furnham, 2016). The HEXACO framework, in which a sixth factor beyond those of the Big Five – honesty-humility – was separately posited as a unique and independent factor (e.g. Ashton et al, 2004a, 2004b; Ashton & Lee, 2007; Lee & Ashton, 2008, 2012). The HEXACO model is perhaps the second most accepted and studied framework beyond the Big Five, and has received attention due to the unique prediction of work outcomes derived from the sixth factor, honesty-humility. Several different Big Seven frameworks have been proposed in both English and non-English languages, to more comprehensively represent the personality domain (e.g. Benet & Waller, 1995; Church et al, 1998; Tellegen & Waller, 1987; Wang et al, 2005), though these models typically receive less attention in the work psychology literature.

Regardless of which trait-based framework one chooses to adopt, it is important to understand that these frameworks describe and organise traits via a hierarchical structure. Taking the Big Five model as an example, the five traits are broad-level factors sitting at a high level of abstraction (or a high bandwidth) in the personality space. Underneath them are less abstract, more specific traits, often called 'facets', and further underneath those facets are narrow-level constructs such as thoughts, feelings and behaviours (e.g. Costa & McCrae, 1995). Understanding personality traits in such a hierarchical structure has important implications in predicting outcomes, as traits at different bandwidths can have different fidelities (e.g. Hogan & Roberts, 1996; Ones & Viswesvaran, 1996). Moreover, for our specific focus on personality change, this hierarchical structure offers important insights for understanding both the extent and the process of how change occurs – a point that will be discussed in more details in later chapters.

Personality at work: research and practice

Research evidence that supports the validity of personality

The emergence and establishment of personality frameworks based on the trait perspective sparked a surge of research interest in studying the implications of personality at work. The establishment of the Big Five as the generally agreed-upon personality structure provided a useful framework to guide many research investigations. Numerous meta-analyses have been conducted since the 1990s highlighting the role of personality in predicting various individually and organisationally important outcomes.

These meta-analyses have found that among the Big Five traits, conscientiousness demonstrates the highest level of validity in predicting employee work performance. Those employees with higher standing in conscientiousness tend to perform better and demonstrate more proficiency at their core tasks (Barrick & Mount, 1991; Barrick et al, 2001; Bartram, 2005; Dudley et al, 2006; Hough, 1992; Hurtz & Donovan, 2000; Salgado, 1997; Tett et al, 1991). These individuals also tend to have a higher 'contextual performance' – the aspect of performance that goes beyond task proficiency, such that they appear to be better organisational citizens in that they help others and contribute to their organisations' welfare (Chiaburu et al, 2011; Dudley et al, 2006; Hurtz & Donovan, 2000; LePine et al, 2002; Organ & Ryan, 1995) and engage less in deviant and counterproductive work behaviours (e.g. theft, lateness, harassment) that may harm their organisations (Berry et al, 2007; Dudley et al, 2006; Salgado, 2002).

Other personality traits also play important roles in employees' work performance. Emotional stability appears to be the second most important trait at work, as emotionally stable employees tend to perform better overall (Hogan & Holland, 2003; Hough, 1992; Hurtz & Donovan, 2000; Salgado, 1997; Tett et al, 1991). Agreeableness appears to be important, especially for the contextual aspect of performance, as those more agreeable tend to be better team players and more readily helpful toward others (Barrick et al, 2001; Bartram, 2005; Chiaburu et al, 2011; Hough, 1992; Hurtz & Donovan, 2000; Hogan & Holland, 2003; Mount et al, 1998). Extraversion seems useful for leadership-related behaviours, which perhaps require more assertiveness and stronger motivation to lead (Barrick et al, 2001; Bartram, 2005; Bono & Judge, 2004; Hogan & Holland, 2003), while openness to experience seems especially important for effectiveness in training and learning settings (Barrick et al, 2001) or for behaviours that relate to creativity and innovation (Bartram, 2005; Hammond et al, 2011; Ma, 2009). Moreover, researchers have found that personality not only matters for work performance and work behaviours, but also for employees' well-being. In particular, emotional stability and extraversion appear to be the most important traits for job satisfaction and for low levels of burnout (see Alarcon et al, 2009; Judge et al, 2002c, for meta-analyses).

There are also fruitful research endeavours to understand the impact of personality using models other than Big Five. For instance, substantial research evidence based on the HEXACO model has shown that the sixth factor, honesty-humility, explains additional variances that are unaccounted for by the Big Five factors (Ashton & Lee, 2019) and has incremental validity over the Big Five traits in predicting work-related outcomes (see Ashton et al, 2014 for a review). Specifically, recent meta-analyses (Pletzer et al, 2019; Lee et al, 2019) provide integrative and empirical evidence that (low) honesty-humility is particularly predictive of counterproductive and deviant work behaviours, and its effect is un-accounted for by any of the Big Five traits. These findings highlight the importance and uniqueness of this sixth personality trait in predicting specific performance criteria.

Researchers have also gone beyond the focus on Big Five and its related personality frameworks to investigate specific personality domains or factors that may be important for work-related outcomes. As an example, proactive personality, which represents individuals' tendency to initiate and enact changes in their environment (Bateman & Crant, 1993), has been highlighted as important in work contexts due to the nature of those employees to improve themselves and their fit with the environment. Meta-analyses (Alarcon et al, 2009; Fuller & Marler, 2009; Thomas et al, 2010; Tornau & Frese, 2013) have suggested that employees with more proactive personalities tend to exhibit higher performance and more career success, and they also tend to be more engaged at work and less likely to experience burnout; this effect was often found to be beyond what was accounted for by the Big Five. Other personality traits that have raised scholarly interest in the work domain include core self-evaluation, which represents individuals' overall tendency to give positive evaluations of themselves (see Judge & Bono, 2001 for a meta-analysis, and Bono & Judge, 2003; Judge & Kammeyer-Mueller, 2011, for reviews), and its related constructs such as self-efficacy (see Stajkovic & Luthans, 1998) and locus of control (see Judge et al, 2002b; Ng et al, 2006; Wang et al, 2010 for meta-analyses), as well as emotion-related constructs such as positive and negative affectivity (see Connolly & Viswesvaran, 2004 for a meta-analysis). While the aforementioned studies focus on either neutral (e.g. Big Five and related) or bright-side personality attributes, scholars have also paid attention to the dark-side or maladaptive personality in the workplace. For instance, the dark triad of personality traits – Machiavellianism, narcissism and psychopathy – were found to be negatively related to job performance and positively related to counterproductive work behaviour (see Grijalva & Newman, 2015; O'Boyle et al, 2012 for meta-analyses). Among these three traits, narcissistic personality appears to have received the most interest, especially for its implications in the context of leadership (see Campbell et al, 2011 for a review). These are just some examples to indicate how personality has been well recognised and investigated in organisational behaviour research.

Given the vast domain of personality research, we are not able to provide comprehensive coverage here concerning all personality factors that have been studied in the work context, hence the review is of the broad strokes only, with the aim of providing foundational knowledge about the key areas concerning personality in work psychology. Interested readers can refer to classic textbooks in this area, which provide a much more comprehensive coverage of different personality dimensions (e.g. Chamorro-Premuzic, 2011; Furnham, 1992; Hogan, 2007). What we can conclude from this brief review is that there is strong and consistent evidence for the predictive validity of personality on a wide range of important work outcomes and across occupational contexts. Although the effect sizes of the individual traits in predicting work criteria have generally not been substantial, mostly around .30 at the maximum, when used collectively, the traits can explain a substantial portion of performance, over and above cognitive ability tests (see Salgado & De Fruyt, 2005, for a review).

Practical application of personality studies in organisations

Knowledge of the predictive validity of personality has been well applied in human resources and organisational development practices. In particular, the commercialisation of personality measurement has contributed to the exponential growth of the testing industry, which is worth somewhere between $500 million and $4 billion (Harrell, 2017; Kinley & Ben-Hur, 2013). Globally, personality tests have been widely used in many organisations across the world. In developed countries such as the US, UK and Australia, up to a third of all organisations use personality tests for talent selection, development, appraisal or other related practices (CIPD, 2017; Di Milia, 2004; Paul, 2004), and the percentage is even higher among large corporations, with the majority of Fortune 500 companies using personality tests in some way.

In particular, using personality testing as part of the personnel selection process has a long history and can be dated back to the early 20th century (Mount & Barrick, 1995), although the more widespread use occurred in the last three decades alongside the establishment of the Big Five model. More importantly, research not only points to the predictive validity of personality testing for work performance, as shown in the meta-analyses, but also highlights that when compared to other established selection methods, such as cognitive ability tests, personality tests demonstrates a good level of incremental validity (see Bartram, 2005; Schmitt et al, 1984; Schmitt & Hunter, 1998 for meta-analyses). It also seems that when adding personality tests to cognitive ability tests, the cumulative predictive validity for work performance can be in the range of .60 to .70 (Salgado & De Fruyt, 2005; Schmitt & Hunter, 1998). This gives us the confidence to use personality tests for personnel selection purposes, especially when combined with other selection practices.

Understanding employees' personalities is also considered crucial for unlocking individuals' potential, which consequently lifts their performance and helps organisations to achieve their goals. Hence, personality testing can also play a substantial role in talent development and retention strategies. As shown by Bartram and Guest (2013), personality can be highly related to individual employees' competency potential – referring to what people could be capable of doing given relevant training and development. Each personality trait indicates that individuals have the potential to excel in different competency potential areas (e.g. extraverted individuals may have higher potential to develop in 'leading and deciding'). Therefore, by assessing and understanding each employee's personality, organisations can craft tailored personal development plans to facilitate career development within organisations.

Personality tests are also used broadly to help team members to develop better awareness of their own and each other's preferences and styles at work, hence unpacking team dynamics and improving team effectiveness. Indeed, as shown by researchers (see Bell, 2007 for a meta-analysis, and LePine et al, 2011, for a review), the composition of individual members' personalities within teams matters for group processes, such as team cohesion and conflict, and thereby impacts team performance.

Overall, personality testing can be used across employees' lifecycles in organisations and can provide useful data that facilitates their performance, well-being, and career development at work.

Personality change: the focus of this book

Thus far we have provided foundational knowledge about the conceptualisation of personality and discussed its critical role in the workplace – both in terms of research evidence and practical applications. However, these existing conceptualisations rest on the premise that personality traits are fixed, enduring entities that do not change – an assumption that has been increasingly challenged over recent decades. Therefore, the authors' intention in this book is to introduce a new, change-oriented perspective on personality and discuss its broad implications for our work and vocational context. The book is organised according to the sections laid out as follows.

Chapter 2 introduces the changing paradigm in our understanding of personality, moving from the fixed-perspective to a malleable perspective of personality. We will review key theoretical developments and summary evidence, primarily from the personality psychology literature, to shed light on why and how personality change can occur throughout our lifespan.

Chapter 3 delves into the topic of how personality can be changed by work and by the broader environment. Building on earlier foundations in organisational psychology and sociology, the authors propose a broad and holistic framework for discussing key drivers of personality change at work. We will review and discuss how the three sources of work experiences – 'What I do', 'Who I work with' and 'How I am doing' – can drive personality change, and also elaborate on how distal environments, including the organisational, societal and international environments, can play a role in facilitating personality change.

Chapter 4 moves away from the focus on how our personality is changed by work – a somewhat passive change process – and introduce a new perspective, demonstrating that personality change can be driven and pursued in a more active manner. In this chapter, the authors discuss how individuals can self-initiate personality change, as well as how organisations can design intervention programmes to actively facilitate personality change.

The final chapter, Chapter 5, brings together existing research and debates to highlight several directions for future research, both in terms of conceptual development as well as methodological considerations. The authors then conclude the chapter with a series of recommendations for how society, organisations and leaders, as well as employees themselves, can actively take on board the concept of personality change in improving work and life.

TWO

Can Personality Traits Change, and How? A Review of Personality Development Literature

Personality is conventionally regarded as a set of stable and enduring individual characteristics that reliably differentiate individuals from one another. For instance, William James (1890, p 126) said that 'in most of us, by the age of thirty, the character has set like plaster, and will never soften again'. McCrae & Costa (2003, p 3) defined traits as 'the basic dispositions that ... endure through adulthood' based on evidence they collected over the years on the longitudinal stability of personality traits. Support for personality stability also comes from genetic studies, providing evidence that the heritability of Big Five traits is in the range of 0.50 ± 0.10 (see Bouchard & Loehlin, 2001, for a review). Theoretically, the stability of personality helps us better understand individuals' attitudes and behaviours at work (see Tasselli et al, 2018, for a review) as we can use personality traits as predictors for a wide range of work outcomes. Practically, the prevalent use of personality testing in personnel selection is being operated under the premise that personality traits are highly stable, and thus that by understanding who our job candidates are we can generate a reasonably reliable prediction as to their behaviour and performance at work once they are employed in the job.

However, is personality truly as stable and fixed as many of us have always believed? Research in personality psychology over recent decades has started to challenge this assumption, and different evidence has emerged that shows an alternative possibility: that personality may be more malleable than we thought. In this chapter, we provide a review of theoretical perspectives on personality change and development. In the following sections, we first discuss changeability of personality and then review key theoretical perspectives from personality psychology literature to discuss why and how personality change occurs throughout our lifespan.

Shifting the paradigm: the changeable nature of personality

If we revisit earlier conceptualisations of personality, we can see that it was never ruled out that traits can be changed. Gordon Allport, the founding father of personality trait research, suggested that people change in response to their social environment: 'The ever-changing nature of traits and their close dependence on the fluid conditions of the environment forbid a conception that is over-rigid or over-simple' (Allport, 1937, p 312). Allport (1961) also commented that people have an inherent drive towards psychological growth. Similarly, Erikson (1950) suggested that adults are just like children in that they mature and change alongside their life stages. In other words, personality change should be expected throughout one's lifespan as it reflects a naturally occurring process towards personal growth and maturation and adaptations to life choices. Other researchers share similar views in that their definition of personality recognises the potential for inconsistency; for instance, Funder (1991, p 36) commented, 'Every global trait is situation specific, in the sense that it is relevant to behaviour in some (perhaps many), but not all, life situations'. From a lifespan development perspective, personality is similarly considered as an open system that constantly interacts with the environment (Baltes, 1997).

When we reflect on our own experiences, it is not difficult to think of how our own personality has been modified by experiences in our life journey. We tend to change our personality during critical life transitions, and some of these are verified by empirical research (see Bleidorn et al, 2018, for a review of personality change due to key life events). For instance, moving beyond student life and entering into the workforce may 'rein' us in to be more conscientious and dependable so that we can perform well in our jobs and be considered good employees (see Specht et al, 2011), while retirement is associated with reduced conscientiousness as we transition out of work-related roles (see Lucas & Donnellan, 2011; Specht et al, 2011). Starting romantic relationships, especially for the first time, may shape us into more emotionally stable people as we acquire these traits in maintaining a happy and healthy relationship (Lehnart et al, 2010; Neyer & Asendorpf, 2001; Neyer & Lehnart, 2007). In a perhaps more dramatic context, going through and surviving traumatic experiences can change our personality and lead to personal growth (Jayawickreme & Blackie, 2014). As we sometimes say, 'What does not kill me makes me stronger'.

Therefore, despite not being the focus in personality psychology since the thriving of the trait-based approach, expecting personality change is quite sensible. Increasing evidence is building up that highlights personality development across the entire lifespan (Roberts et al, 2006; Orth et al, 2012; Specht et al, 2011), and studies tracking individuals from childhood to mid- and late-life suggested that lifelong stability of personality is quite low, with the highest correlation only around .20 (Hampson & Goldberg, 2006; Harris et al, 2016). Personality change can extend into our late life stages, with some evidence even pointing to reduced stability in older ages (Lucas & Donnellan, 2011; Specht et al, 2011). Such salience of change in old age 'directly refutes the argument that either personality traits do not change or the changes that are demonstrated are governed entirely by genetic mechanisms' (Roberts & Wood, 2006, p 20). Furthermore, even the biological perspective that provides strong support to personality stability may need reconsidering, as Roberts (2018, p 23) suggested that 'though DNA is fixed at conception, the expression of DNA can be modified and reprogrammed by experiences in the environment'. Therefore, personality being based on biological mechanisms doesn't mean that it is fixed and unchangeable (Bleidorn et al, 2019).

On another front, if we refer to the area of clinical psychology, we see a very different perspective on personality change. Clinical psychologists and psychotherapists have long been interested in the opposite research question as compared to personality researchers; that is, rather than uncovering why people change, their research question is more about why people do not change. Their assumption is that people can enact positive changes in various domains in their lives, and personality change should occur as a result of clinical intervention. Those not changing – who would be otherwise considered 'stable' by personality researchers – might instead be considered as resistant to change (e.g. Pervin, 1994).

Approaching personality as changeable rather than stable represents a major paradigm shift in organisational research, as this requires us to treat personality as an outcome, rather than as a predictor, of work-related variables (Tasselli et al, 2018; Woods et al, 2013). This is not an easy shift for organisational research, which has a long tradition of relying on the fixed, trait-based perspective of personality. More than a decade ago, at a time when the personality change perspective was taking off, Roberts (2006, p 5) commented that, despite organisational and work psychology having shown great interest and advancement in personality research, 'the version of personality psychology adopted in organisational psychology has proven to be overly static.' This static perspective persists, as when Woods et al conducted a review of personality change and its influence on work, they concluded that 'there are almost no studies that examine the reciprocal effects of personality and work in the IWO [industrial, work and organizational psychology] literature' (Woods et al, 2013, p 19). However, the perspective has shifted since then, with an increasing number of researchers taking on the task of understanding how work changes personality, often through the use of large-scale panel data which makes such endeavours possible (e.g. Li et al, 2014, 2019; Wille et al, 2012; Wille et al, 2019; Wu, 2016; Wu & Griffin, 2012; Wu et al, 2015; Wu et al, 2020). We will review more details on these studies in Chapter 3.

What changes are in place?

When it comes to personality change, it is necessary to recognise that different types of change exist. In particular, research in this area tends to focus on three types of change: mean-level change, rank-order change and individual difference in change (De Fruyt et al, 2006; Specht et al, 2014; Morey & Hopwood, 2013; Caspi et al, 2005; Roberts et al, 2008).

Mean-level change concerns whether the entire population experiences increase or decrease in personality change over time, typically examined through standardised mean differences between different time points. Many studies have suggested that as a whole population we experience an increase in personality traits over time that reflect greater maturity, such as conscientiousness, emotional stability and agreeableness (Roberts et al, 2006; Roberts & Mroczek, 2008), as we describe in the next section.

Rank-order change is also relevant to the entire population, as it concerns the stability or change of the relative placement of individuals within groups (that is, do individuals currently ranked high in agreeableness, as compared to others, remain high in agreeableness later on). This is often ascertained by test-retest correlations. In this regard, researchers have found that while there is a moderate level of rank-order stability from childhood to adulthood, such stability is far from total, especially over long intervals (Damien et al, 2019; Fraley & Roberts, 2005; Roberts & DelVecchio, 2000).

Finally, individual difference in change captures the individual's unique journey in personality development. For instance, although normative development takes place in the direction towards higher conscientiousness for the entire population, there exist substantial differences across individuals, such that some people may remain at the same level while others even show a decrease in this trait (Bleidorn, 2012; Borghuis et al, 2017). This is sometimes referred to as interindividual difference in intraindividual change (Mroczek et al, 2006). All these ways of looking at change are important, and different studies often come with a different focus in relation to the type of change.

Why does personality change take place?

If personality does change throughout our life journey, why? While many perspectives have been proposed, the most widely discussed and accepted perspective is the neo-socioanalytical theory, a holistic model proposed by Roberts and colleagues for understanding personality development and continuity (Roberts, 2006; Roberts & Wood, 2006). This theory incorporates both the trait-based perspective, which assumes stability of personality, and the social interactionist perspective, which conceptualises personality as shaped by social context. It articulates several critical principles in explaining why personality changes due to normative and non-normative events and towards increased maturity. Given the prominence of this model in the current personality change literature, we will further examine the most widely discussed principles covered in this theory while incorporating other relevant literature. We also want to stress that this is not a comprehensive review of all theoretical propositions, yet the perspectives elaborated on later appear to be the most robust and widely discussed in the personality change literature in recent years. Interested readers can refer to 'What Drives Adult Personality Development? A Comparison of Theoretical Perspectives and Empirical Evidence' (Specht et al, 2014) for a review of other theories, and 'A critical evaluation of the Neo-Socioanalytic Model of personality' (Roberts & Nickel, 2017) for a critical discussion of other personality development principles that have been discussed but for which evidence may be relatively less robust.

Age-related change and the maturity principle

As human beings we grow with age, and such growth can move in the direction towards greater maturity. Maturity can be an ambiguous term, but it broadly describes how individuals develop in the direction that enables them to be more psychologically healthy and fulfilled (Josefsson et al, 2013). In the research on human development, it has been observed that with age we become more other-oriented, more committed to mutual and interdependent relationship with others (Erikson, 1950; Franz & White, 1985; Levinson et al, 1978). Research has shown that, compared to early adulthood, adults in mid-life stages tend to be more concerned with issues of generativity – issue relating to the well-being of the next generation (Erikson, 1950) – as well as being more realistic, recognising their own limitations, and intensely attached (Levinson et al, 1978).

In recent decades, empirical evidence regarding personality is accumulating that tracks and profiles how such maturity increases over our entire lifespan. Summarising a great deal of research evidence, Roberts and colleagues (Roberts et al, 2006; Roberts & Mroczek, 2008) reported that from age 10 to age 70+, mean-level change in personality was remarkable. As we age, we steadily increase our standing especially in the traits of conscientiousness, emotional stability and agreeableness. The cumulative change across the entire lifespan in these traits is close to one standard deviation, which is a rather large effect size in psychology. The development of these traits is considered to be in line with maturity, as mature individuals tend to be more responsible, self-controlled, warm and considerate. For instance, traits related to conscientiousness help us to perform well in our life tasks through our striving towards goals and persisting despite failures; traits related to emotional stability help us to live with greater self-awareness of our emotions and to manage them effectively; traits related to agreeableness enable us to have rewarding and trusting relationships with others and to enjoy more satisfactory social lives. In sum, desirable traits are those that can facilitate one's optimal functioning as a productive member in society, representing 'functional maturity' (Hogan & Roberts, 2004). This trend of trait growth is described as the 'maturity principle' of personality development (Roberts & Wood, 2006; Roberts, 2006), describing how personality changes in a socially desirable fashion that helps individuals better adapt to the world. The three traits, emotional stability, conscientiousness and agreeableness, are also the traits that can be subsumed under a common higher-order factor, termed 'stability' (as opposed to 'plasticity') (Digman, 1997; DeYoung, 2006, and 2010), as the three traits help to regulate emotional, motivational and social stability respectively. Coupled with the maturity perspective, this means that the stability meta-trait of our personality increases alongside age.

The maturity principle has received support from various cross-cultural studies, such as in the US, Germany, Italy and Finland (see Roberts & Nickel, 2017, for a review), thus showing the robustness of this principle in that the human maturation process can be universal. It is also worth highlighting that most changes in these traits appeared to occur during ages 20–60 (Roberts & Mroczek, 2008), which coincide with the critical period of individuals' working lives. This indicates the possibility that work may be an important source of personality change.

It is necessary however to mention that the previously discussed perspective on functional maturity reflects the adjustment aspect of maturity rather than the growth aspect of maturity – a point made by researchers Staudinger and Kunzmann. They suggested that adjustment is about mastering the environment and adapting to societal circumstances (for example, norms, rules and expectations) to increase the individuals' functionality in society, while growth focuses more on developing intrapersonal attributes such as virtues, insights, self-transcendence and wisdom. While these two can be related, 'adjustment is by no means a sufficient condition for growth' (Staudinger & Kunzmann, 2005, p 321). In relation to personality change towards greater maturity, while the improvement in adjustment can be made in our dealing with life-related tasks (a point discussed in the following section), the improvement in growth is much more difficult to achieve, and perhaps only likely to happen after extremely stressful or traumatic events (post-traumatic growth). Indeed, empirical research on personality change tends to focus on, and provide evidence for, the former rather than the latter type of maturity, and researchers have indeed suggested that growth does not necessarily happen in one's lifespan (Caspi et al, 2005).

It is also worth noting that although much of the evidence we have reviewed tends to suggest positive change (that is, change towards greater maturity), change does not necessarily happen in a positive direction. For instance, some evidence suggests that when transiting to parenthood, personality change can take place in a maladaptive way, such as a decrease in conscientiousness, emotional stability, agreeableness (Hutteman et al, 2014) and self-esteem (Bleidorn et al, 2016), especially immediately after the birth of the first child. Studying change thus requires us to consider the direction of change, including non-linear and reverse directions.

Normative and non-normative change and the social investment principle

People change their personality in response to the vast amount of life events that we are confronted with. Some events can be normative and age-related, such as establishing a career, selecting a partner and developing intimate relationships, forming a family and raising children, coping with an empty nest and adjusting to the physical decline from middle age, among others. Some other events can be independent of age, and represent individuals' unique life journeys, such as moving abroad, joining the army, taking up volunteering work and coping with unemployment, among others. Both these normative and non-normative events can present new demands in our lives, which call for personality change.

Roberts and colleagues (Roberts, 2006; Roberts & Wood, 2006; Roberts et al, 2005) articulated this in the 'social investment principle' of the neo-socioanalytical theory, partly to explain why human maturation occurs in line with age. With this principle, they pointed out that the way social context influences personality change is primarily achieved through individuals' investment in social roles. By being forced to confront and cope with the demands of social roles (for example, being a partner, a parent, a useful employee or a respected leader), individuals develop new identities and adapt themselves to be in line with the new roles' expectations. Specifically, as discussed and tested by Roberts and colleagues, when people commit to social institutions, they are exposed to the contingencies contained in the social roles, and such contingencies come with role expectations which call for appropriate behaviours to fulfil such roles. These role expectations can be powerful motivators, such that conforming behaviours are likely to be rewarded and behaviours violating these expectations might be punished, partly through interactions with and feedback from other social members. In this way, behaviours in line with role expectations are continuously elicited and reinforced, leading to personality change. Investment in social roles can occur in multiple domains, such as family, work or religion, and meta-analysis revealed that all these investments lead to positive change in our personality, such as increases in agreeableness, conscientiousness and emotional stability (Lodi-Smith & Roberts, 2007).

Many of the social roles induced by life tasks are normative, universal and promoted by our modern culture, such as entering into employment, getting married and having children, which thus indicates that all people go through similar life transitions and that there should be convergence across cultures in terms of personality development trajectories. Yet it is necessary to recognise that social roles can also be shaped and constructed by culture, and thus that cross-cultural differences should be expected. For instance, different cultures may have somewhat different 'social clocks' (Neugarten et al, 1965) which define the normative timing of life transitions. This resulted in an age effect on personality change, as in some cultures individuals tend to take on adult responsibilities, such as starting careers and families, at an earlier age. Bleidorn et al (2013) empirically tested whether personality change in different cultures is associated with the normative timing of adult role transitions. Using a large-scale, web-based sample of young adults (16–40 years old) in 62 countries, they found that, first, across countries, age had a significant relationship with all Big Five personality traits, and that the effect was larger with traits that are associated with functional maturity, namely conscientiousness, agreeableness and neuroticism. This supports the notion that personality maturation is a universal phenomenon. Second, and more importantly, cultural differences in the age effect were observed, such that cultures with earlier normative timing for the transition into job roles was associated with a decrease in neuroticism and increases in conscientiousness, agreeableness and openness. Surprisingly, the normative timing of the transition into family roles had much less impact on personality change. The researchers speculated that job roles might present more prescriptive and strict demands on individuals, while the family roles might allow more leeway and freedom. This research might lend some support to the conception of the work domain as a more important context for personality change. Researchers have also discussed other culturally unique factors influencing personality change. For instance, gender differences in personality might present different patterns across cultures, as in some, such as in Western societies, women may be afforded more roles than in other cultures. Religions that dominate the norms in certain cultures can also impact the expectations and demands placed on individuals, thus shaping the personality development of individuals in these societies (Roberts & Wood, 2006).

Moreover, changes in personality can be caused by non-normative events that happen to individuals. Some of these events can be beyond individuals' control and emerge in a random manner (for example, relocating to a new place or losing a loved one), while others may be influenced by individuals themselves (for example, choosing a job) (Fraley & Roberts, 2005). Regardless of the causes, these idiosyncratic life journeys enable individuals to change and develop in unique patterns. This type of change is referred to as individual difference in change, and can be invisible if we only focus on group-level changes such as those associated with the maturation process or normative events (Roberts et al, 2003; Roberts et al, 2008). In relation to this change, individuals' work and vocational experience can be an important source of non-normative events that cause personality change. For instance, those who joined the army tend to reduce their agreeableness compared to civilians, possibly due to the military context calling for fast reactions and assertive decision-making, which are characteristics opposed to agreeableness (Jackson et al, 2012b). As another example, women's life choice tends to change their personalities, as those women who participate more actively in the labour force and who achieve more occupational success tend to have increased self-confidence, independence and self-assertion (Clausen & Gilens, 1990; Roberts, 1997). Furthermore, college students with different vocational interests tend to carve out different personality development trajectories (Lüdtke et al, 2011; Wille et al, 2012; Wille & De Fruyt, 2014). For instance, those exhibiting early investment and participation in 'directorial' or 'inspiratory' roles reduce their personality agreeableness over time, possibly due to that decreased agreeableness being preferred and thus developed as individuals fulfil these roles (Wille et al, 2012). We will discuss such personality change caused by individuals' unique experiences and perceptions at work in more details in Chapter 3.

The corresponsive principle and the reciprocal effect of selection and socialisation

Roberts and colleagues (Robert & Wood, 2006; Roberts et al, 2003) proposed a 'corresponsive principle' in person-ality change, which highlights that people are drawn into life experiences (for example, jobs and careers) that fit with their pre-existing characteristics, thus people's personality devel-opment is deepened and reinforced by their characteristics. For instance, an extravert is more likely than an introvert to choose and stay in a job that requires a high level of extra-version, such as salesperson, and such a job will in turn make them more extraverted, reinforcing their existing personality. This process has also been described as a reciprocal relationship between the 'selection effect', which describes how individ-uals self-select into certain contexts due to their current per-sonality and thus shape their context to be in line with their personality, and the 'socialisation effect', whereby contextual conditions can impact individuals, developing and changing their personality (Holland, 1997; Roberts et al, 2012; Specht et al, 2011). Such a reciprocal effect is in line with the broader person–environment interaction perspective (Bandura, 2001; Schneider, 1987), and has thus been the focus for work and organisational psychologists in studying personality change, with recent empirical research consistently pointing to the co-existence of both mechanisms (Denissen et al, 2014;

Le et al, 2014; Li et al, 2014, 2019; Sutin et al, 2009; Wille & De Fruyt, 2014; Wille et al, 2019; Wu & Griffin, 2012).

What should be noted is that the corresponsive principle and selection vs. socialisation effect mostly speak to an amplifying and deepening effect of environment on individuals' existing personality traits, leading to positive feedback loops and gain spirals (Caspi et al, 2005). Empirical research provides support for this principle (as tested and discussed in the aforementioned studies), yet also reveals that it does not always hold true. For example, in studies by Li et al (2014, 2019), which involved a number of work characteristics, the reciprocal, reinforcing effect between work characteristics and personality traits were only found for some variables but not others; for instance, between job demand, job control and proactive personality (Li et al, 2014), and between job insecurity and dispositional optimism (Li et al, 2019), but not for other work characteristics such as social support. In Wille et al's study (2019), which tested whether climbing the corporate ladder can amplify an increase in narcissism – a dark-side personality trait – the authors found that people with steep career growth in the first stage of their careers actually experienced smaller growth in narcissism in the next career stage. All in all, it seems that the effect of environment on personality is complex and cannot be completely subsumed under a deepening effect.

The corresponsive principle tends to focus on the fit between personality and environment and the reinforcing effect of environment on existing personality, while suggesting that a misfit between personality and environment will result in alienation such that individuals will attempt to escape a prolonged exposure to such an experience (Roberts et al, 2003). However, it is important to recognise that even when a misfit occurs, rather than taking an avoidant approach, people can choose to transform their job experiences, such as by modifying their environment, shifting their attention or reappraising their experiences so that their environment better suits their needs and the personality-environment misfit can be reduced

(Denissen et al, 2013; Stoll & Trautwein, 2017; Roberts, 2006; Woods et al, 2013; Woods et al, 2019). A number of theoretical models of personality change at work, as we discuss in the following section, provide a more detailed elaboration on such a process.

The self-regulatory process in personality change

The previously discussed theoretical perspectives might give the impression that personality change occurs largely through a relatively passive process that is subject to the natural setting, environmental factors and life experiences. However, the important role of our agentic selves should be underscored, as it can be the most important driving force of personality change (Denissen et al, 2013; Specht et al, 2014a). For instance, the selection effect, as we have discussed, highlights that individuals can apply their initiatives and agency in either selecting themselves into or out of certain environments, and in their crafting of the environment. The 'maturity principle' and 'social investment principle' can be underpinned by individuals' internalisation of social roles and their conscious learning and practices in coping with new demands.

While earlier research has noticed the importance of goals and desires in personality change (Roberts et al, 2004), it was not until more recently that the self-regulatory mechanism in personality change was purposefully conceptualised (Denissen et al, 2013; Hennecke et al, 2014). Denissen et al (2013, p 255) suggested that trait-relevant behaviours are performed because they are 'strategic means to desired end states', and that people can engage in various forms of self-regulatory strategies when interacting with their environment, including selecting or de-selecting their situations, modifying situational features, directing attention away from undesirable features in the situations, changing their appraisals of the situations and suppressing undesirable impulses towards the situations. They also suggested that personal goals and social norms can serve as the 'reference values' that motivate individuals' self-regulation with regard to change. Hennecke et al (2014) took a functional perspective in disentangling this process, proposing to focus on goals people attempt to achieve in changing their trait-relevant behaviours, and how self-regulatory efforts enable the sustaining of such change. In doing so, they proposed a three-part framework to articulate the three preconditions of personality change, with the first two preconditions focusing on the motivation and commitment to change, represented by the perceived *value* (desirability) and *valence* (feasibility) of change, and the third precondition focused on turning such a change into habit (that is, the change becoming habitual) so that a stable personality shift occurs. The volitional and intentional personality change perspective has gained more traction over recent years, such that a series of research endeavours, including cross-cultural studies, have been dedicated to understanding how individuals can actively set goals towards personality change (Baranski, 2018; Baranski et al, 2020; Baranski et al, 2017; Geukes et al, 2018; Hudson & Roberts, 2014; Hudson & Fraley, 2015; 2016b; Hudson et al, 2020; Robinson et al, 2015).

The self-regulatory process is especially useful for understanding why and how individuals differ in personality change, and is also useful for us as organisational researchers to develop effective strategies to support individuals through their change journey. This perspective, as well as the key factors in the self-regulatory process towards personality change, will be elaborated in more detail in Chapter 4.

How does personality change occur at a microanalytical level?

The lifespan development perspective of personality change, as we discussed in the previous section, focuses mostly on the broad *macro-analytical* level as it discusses how changes occur at a structural level. However, how does personality change take place on a more *micro-analytical* level through our momentary and temporary experiences? Comparatively, this area is much less discussed (Bleidorn, 2012; Geukes et al, 2018), yet several recent discussions converge on a bottom-up change process whereby short-term change, at the personality-state level, unfolds over time and eventually turns into long-term change at the trait level.

Roberts and colleagues (Roberts & Jackson, 2008; Roberts, 2009; for updated discussions see Roberts, 2018) were among the first to suggest a bottom-up change process, using the sociogenomic model of personality to articulate how such change occurs. Roberts suggested that the way environmental factors change trait-level personality is through repeatedly eliciting state-level personality change; for instance, students prefer their professors to be more organised, and this may lead professors to change their behaviour to be in line with that expectation; these behaviours are rewarded, such as through students' positive evaluations, and thereby reinforced over time. Through this slow, incremental process induced by prolonged environmental influence, neuroanatomical changes in brain structure could occur and new personality traits will be born. In other words, states act as the mediators for the effect of environment on personality traits to occur.

A theoretical framework called TESSERA was recently developed to unpack this process in more depth (Wrzus & Roberts, 2017). TESSERA refers to a process of Triggering situations, Expectancy, States/State Expressions and ReActions. *Triggering situations*, referring to events or situations (for example, life events, social roles or interventions), can trigger *expectations* in individuals as to how to behave, feel or think, which enables individuals to select their responses and thus activate a *state/state expression*. Such an expression will cause subsequent *reactions*, which can either come from oneself (for example, through emotions) or from others (for example, through feedback). The TESSERA sequence represents the reactive process towards a single event or situation; therefore, for long-term personality change to occur, the same sequence needs to be repeated so that reflection and learning-related processes can take place.

Such a bottom-up process is broadly supported in other conceptualisations of personality change (Geukes et al, 2018; Bleidorn et al, 2019), including those that were aimed at understanding personality change through active intervention (Allemand & Flückiger, 2017; Chapman et al, 2014) rather than through naturally occurring processes. It is also in line with prominent models in which personality is conceptualised as a density distribution of states (Fleeson, 2001; 2004), which provide insights for us for understanding personality changes via the shift of the entire distribution. Empirical research that directly tests how such a process works, however, is sparse, as such studies can be very costly as they involve intensive data collection (Bleidorn et al, 2019). Furthermore, alternative perspectives have been proposed, with researchers recognising that, first, the bottom-up process may result in only short-term change rather than permanent change once the triggering environment is removed; and second, permanent changes could take place without a bottom-up pathway, such as when individuals encounter highly stressful or traumatic events (Bleidorn et al, 2018; Roberts, 2018). Needless to say, continuous development of the personality change process is required both conceptually and empirically.

Summary

In this chapter, we provide a broad-stroke overview on the what, why and how of personality change, largely drawing from existing literature in the personality psychology discipline, which has embraced the change perspective of personality at this time, while new theories are continuously being developed. In comparison, research on personality change in the work setting is comparatively less dominant; yet growing awareness and acceptance of this perspective shows promising prospects. In the next two chapters, we first consider personality change as naturally induced by the work environment and the broader, organisational, societal and international environment (Chapter 3), and then explain how individuals and organisations can be active agents in facilitating personality change (Chapter 4).

THREE

How Work Experiences Drive Personality Change: The Impact of Work, Organisational, Societal and International Environment

In this chapter we seek to identify work-related factors that shape personality change. We focus on changes occurring in individuals' personalities as a result of their work and employment experiences and of the socialising pressure of normative demands arising during these experiences – that is, the 'socialisation effect'. To offer a broad overview, we seek to identify drivers in the work, organisational and societal environment, including factors at the work level (for example, work and vocational characteristics, leadership and achievement), the organisational level (organisational structure and culture, among others) and the broader societal level (changing technology in the workplace, increasingly precarious employment, delayed retirement age and cultural changes are a few examples). To achieve the goal of this chapter, we take three steps, which also reflect the structure of this chapter.

First, we provide a brief review of traditions in organisational and social psychology regarding the study of work and personality change. While studies of personality development have emerged in personality psychology in last few decades (see Chapter 2), the role of the work environment in shaping personality change has also been well recognised in both organisational psychology (see Brousseau, 1983; Frese, 1982) and social psychology (see House, 1981; Jokela, 2017; McLeod & Lively, 2006; Ryff, 1987). We seek to incorporate these traditions into our discussion. Second, based on knowledge derived from personality, organisational and social psychology, we propose a holistic framework to help identify key drivers in the work, organisational and societal environment, and illustrate how they could act as proximal and distal drivers for personality change. Third, we use the proposed framework to review what is already known in the literature and elaborate on what more needs to be explored to advance the understanding of work and personality change.

Traditional understanding of work and personality change in organisational and social psychology

Organisational psychologists, particularly scholars studying work design, have argued that job experiences and work characteristics can change people's temperament or personality (Frese, 1982; Hall & Las Heras, 2010; Parker & Turner, 2002). The German action theory, for example, considers humans as active beings who develop and change through action (Frese & Zapf, 1994). Frese and colleagues (Frese, 1982; Frese & Zapf, 1994) argued that specific work designs impose different cognitive, emotional and behavioural requirements, which necessitate that employees engage in actions that are consistent with these requirements. In this way, work influences personality development as the work environment and experiences shape one's values, social roles and activities on a daily basis (Frese, 1982). Similarly, Parker and Turner (2002) argued that, over the long term, work design could affect motivationally oriented individual traits, such as aspiration or self-esteem, as individuals adapt themselves to fit with their situations. They claimed that 'work design might thus have more profound and long-lasting motivational effects than we have assumed until now' (Parker & Turner, 2002, p 80). In an article linking research on job design and career theory, Hall and Las Heras (2010) refer to 'smart jobs', jobs with work characteristics that can enhance individuals' adaptive capacities and self-identities (for example, those that promote protean career orientations and introduce new possible selves). A good number of recent studies on work and personality change are based on this tradition (Li et al, 2014, 2019; Wille & De Fruyt, 2014; Woods et al, 2020; Wu, 2016; Wu & Griffin, 2012; Wu et al, 2015).

In social psychology, studies on social structure and personality have traditionally viewed individuals as being embedded in different layers of social structure (see Kohn, 1989; McLeod & Lively, 2006). As such, not only can individuals shape social structure via their behaviours and activities, either individually or collectively, but social structure can also shape individuals' beliefs, attitudes, emotional responses and actions, or personality – if those entities become individuals' 'stable and persisting psychological attributes' (a broad conception of personality) (House, 1981, p 527). In this tradition, social structure has been defined as 'a *persisting* and bounded *pattern* of social relationships (or pattern of behavioural intention) among the units (persons or positions) in a social system' (House, 1981, p 542, emphasis in the original). As elaborated by McLeod and Lively (2006, p 77), social structure 'encompasses features of the macro-social order such as the structure of the labour market and systems of social stratification as well as processes such as industrialisation'. In addition to social structure, culture has been discussed and recognised as another important force that both shapes and is shaped by individuals' personalities (Kohn et al, 2000; Ryff, 1987). Studies based on this tradition were mainly conducted in the 1980s by Kohn and his colleagues (see Spenner, 1988), who sought to understand whether social stratification can shape one's personality via occupational choice and work characteristics. Drawing on this tradition to advance personality development studies has been encouraged in recent years (Jokela, 2017).

Both traditions contribute to the understanding of work and personality development. Whilst the tradition from organisational psychology focuses on how work and vocational characteristics shape individuals, and has driven many research endeavours in recent years, the tradition from social psychology offers a broader lens, in that it not only covers broader factors but also acknowledges a bi-directional influence between person and environment, thus helping to extend the scope of examinations of work and personality development.

A framework for identifying drivers of personality change in work, organisational and societal contexts

Based on the foundation of personality, organisational and social psychology, we propose a schematic framework (Figure 3.1) to help identify drivers of personality change in work, organisational and societal contexts, and to illustrate how these drivers can broadly impact personality change. Our framework is intended to offer a holistic view rather than a fine-grained illustration of all possible drivers and processes of personality change. In the following sections we first introduce this framework and then discuss key factors in work, organisational and societal contexts in more detail.

First, our framework acknowledges that personality change results from psychological processes relating to one's self-understanding, feelings and behaviours (the rightmost part of Figure 3.1). These processes have been recognised in the previous literature on personality development, such as in the neo-socioanalytical theory (Roberts & Wood, 2006) and the TESSERA model (Wrzus & Roberts, 2017) as were reviewed in Chapter 2. These processes help to explain how the work environment can drive personality change in empirical studies (Li et al, 2014; Wu, 2016; Wu et al, 2020). Our framework

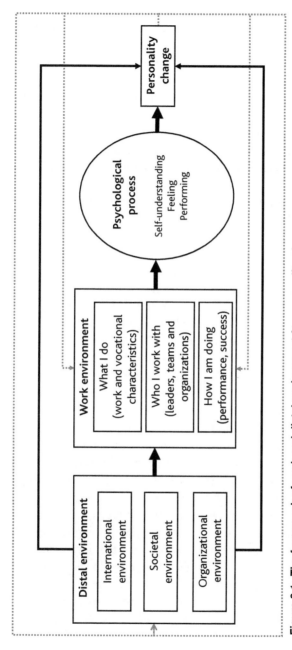

Figure 3.1: The framework of work and distal environment for personality change

acknowledges the diversity and complexity of the psychological mechanisms underlying personality development.

Second, we propose that the work environment is a proximal environment that can shape the psychological processes towards personality change. We further identify three important sources of work experiences within the work environment, including 'What I do', 'Who I work with' and 'How I am doing at work', which cover structural, social and evaluative experiences at work. The first source (that is, 'What I do') concerns task, job or vocational characteristics, or those aspects that determine one's job content and the ways of performing that job. The second source ('Who I work with') concerns relational factors that can influence one's activities at work, such as influences from supervisors and colleagues and factors that indicate employees' relationship with their organisations. The third source ('How I am doing at work') relates to one's evaluative experience of work performance, such as objective or subjective job success. The effects of the different sources of work experiences on personality change have been examined in different studies in a piecemeal fashion, without systematic integration. Our framework, by acknowledging all three sources, seeks to bring scattered discussions together, and to summarise what we know so far and how we can further advance research in this area.

Third, our framework examines influence on personality change from a multilevel perspective. Beyond the immediate work context, we acknowledge the effect of the organisational, societal and international environment in shaping one's personality change, either directly or indirectly, via work experiences. This conceptualisation highlights the need to consider factors at different contextual levels, and unpacks how higher-level, distal factors (factors in the organisational, societal and international environments for example) can influence one's work experiences and personality change. This acknowledgement follows the tradition of social psychology by considering different layers of environment when examining the relationship between environment and people. We recognise that our framework is oversimplified, as the dynamics between different environmental layers have not been properly depicted. However, our focus is not on these specific dynamics; rather, our intention is to expand the scope of studies.

Such a multilevel influence suggests that a specific societal culture can shape how organisations are designed and operated, which then determines the work environment in those organisations, and further influences how employees behave at work. For instance, organisations in Japan and the UK are different in terms of how they design and implement organisational structures, how they manage employment relationships and how they conduct business in general, due to their very different cultures (Lincoln & McBride, 1987). Societal culture can also influence how people select and approach their work or occupation, and how they define success at work. We also cannot ignore the influence of global change and significant events on one's work and thereby on one's personality. For example, technological change, such as the use of artificial intelligence and robots across different industries, can change the employment landscape – reducing jobs in some areas while creating new jobs in others, and telecommuting, or telework, in which cyber interactions become critical to one's work life, can directly shape people's work experiences. Events on a global scale can also create significant change in one's work, including, for example, civil wars that cause disruptions in societies and large-scale international migration of refugees, trade tensions between countries that cause job loss and industrial change, and pandemics (for example, COVID-19) that impact many businesses as well as people's work globally.

Finally, our framework acknowledges the influence in turn of personality change on environment (depicted by the grey dot lines in Figure 3.1). This acknowledgement is in line with the broader understanding of individuals' active role in their environment. For example, personality has been found to influence one's choice of occupation (Barrick et al, 2003), interactions with supervisors and colleagues (Chiaburu et al, 2011) and work performance (Barrick & Mount, 1991; Bono & Vey, 2007). Personality, especially the founders' personality, impacts businesses' organisational culture and leads to the attraction and retention of people with similar dispositional styles (Schneider, 1987). Personality can also play a role in shaping business and economic activities in the broader region. For instance, Florida (2002) suggested that creative people move to creative cities (Austin and Seattle in 1990s are two examples) and thereby drive larger economic growth in those regions in comparison to cities that could not attract these people (Pittsburgh and Cleveland for instance).

Work environment and personality change

We now focus on the three sources of work experiences in turn ('What I do', 'Who I work with' and 'How I am doing'). Collectively, these sources capture different demands in the work environment that can drive personality change. A demand–induced mechanism of personality change is well articulated by Woods et al (2019), who proposed a demands–affordances transactional model in unpacking this mechanism. Specifically, they suggested that workplaces can impose multiple levels of demands on individuals (at the job, vocational, team/group and organisational levels), and that these demands call upon personality as a personal resource (an 'affordance') in response, leading to the activation of relevant traits. The transactions between demands and affordances take place in a way that increases the fit between individuals and their environment. When there is a fit between demands and personality (for example, an extraverted person entering a job that requires extraversion), the developmental mechanism functions such that the relevant trait is activated and reinforced. When there is a misfit between demands and personality (as when an introverted person enters a job that requires extraversion), individuals may need to act in ways that are atypical of their traits in order to adjust to such demands. In this case, as new behaviours are practiced and reinforced through a learning process, trait-level change could occur, and a better person–environment fit could then be achieved. The idea of person–environment fit and misfit, and their implication in personality change, was further spelled out in Woods et al's (2020) conceptualisation of vocational gravitation and vocational inhabitation, which respectively represent situations in which individuals self-select into certain environments and in which such self-selection is not possible. Here we summarise what we know from the literature in relation to how each of the three sources impact personality change.

What do I do? Work and vocational characteristics and personality change

The function of work and vocational characteristics in shaping one's personality has been discussed since the 1970s. The general idea behind this line of research is that work and vocational characteristics define specific work roles and tasks that can shape one's cognition, emotion and behaviour at work in particular directions. If such an impact consistently occurs to individuals, their temporary cognitive, emotional and behavioural reactions can gradually become stable and idiosyncratic characteristics, as illustrated in the TESSERA framework (Wrzus & Roberts, 2017) (see Chapter 2). We first review studies on work characteristics and then discuss studies on vocational characteristics.

Work characteristics

Work characteristics are the specific features of jobs that describe what an individual is requested to do when performing a specific job. A classical framework of work characteristics is the job characteristics model proposed by Hackman and Oldham (1975, 1976), who identified five core job characteristics: skill variety (whether an individual needs to apply different skills to complete their work), task identity (whether an individual can complete tasks from beginning to end, as opposed to doing only a piece of them), task significance (whether an individual can see a positive impact on others resulting from their work), job autonomy (whether an individual can determine what their tasks are, as well as how and when to do them), and feedback (whether an individual has knowledge about how well they are doing in their tasks). Hackman and Oldham also proposed and found that these five core job characteristics can induce psychological states – such as a sense of meaningfulness, felt responsibility and knowledge of results due to own efforts – which in turn effect one's intrinsic motivation and work performance. The job demands-resources model (Demerouti et al, 2001; Karasek et al, 1998; Karasek, 1979; Schaufeli & Bakker, 2004) is another well-known framework that focuses on the balance between demands – such as workload and time pressure – and resources –such as job control (or autonomy) and social support – and the individual's consequent stress experiences and physical/mental health. In brief, both models uncover important work characteristics, though the former puts more emphasis on the effect of work characteristics on work motivation, while the latter focuses more on how work characteristics impact stress and health. To date, the scope of work characteristics has been expanded to include task, cognitive, social, emotional and physical environment characteristics (see Grant & Parker, 2009; Humphrey et al, 2007; Morgeson & Humphrey, 2006).

Studies on work characteristics and personality change vary in their choice of the specific variables being investigated. Regarding work characteristics, some examine the five characteristics identified in the job characteristics model (Brousseau, 1978; Brousseau & Prince, 1981), some focus on work characteristics under the job demands or job resources categories (Sutin & Costa, 2010; Wu, 2016), while others select only one or a few work characteristics depending on their research interests (Kohn & Schooler, 1978, 1982; Li et al, 2014, 2019; Wu et al, 2015). Regarding personality, some focus on changes in all the Big Five traits (Sutin & Costa, 2010; Wu, 2016), while many others focus on specific traits, such as locus of control (Wu et al, 2015), proactive personality (Li et al, 2014), trait optimism (Li et al, 2019), intellectual flexibility (Kohn & Schooler, 1973), self-directedness (Kohn & Schooler, 1982) or self-concept (Gecas & Seff, 1989; Mortimer & Lorence, 1979). Such diverse examinations, on the one hand, offer rich evidence about the impact of work characteristics on personality, but on the other make it difficult to develop an integrative knowledge base.

Studies also vary in their research design. Although several studies in the 1970s and '80s started to examine the impact of work and vocational characteristics on personality, research design in some of those early studies unfortunately had several drawbacks that prevented the researchers from drawing conclusions. For example, some studies (Gecas & Seff, 1989; Kohn, 1976; Kohn & Schooler, 1973) relied on cross-sectional data, which cannot disentangle the direction of effect between work and personality. We will discuss research design issues specifically in Chapter 5. In the following section we summarise studies that used proper longitudinal designs.

Despite the focus on different work characteristics and personality traits, scholars share the view that stimulating jobs, or jobs with high degrees of autonomy and complexity that require employees to deal with a wide range of data, tasks and people and that allow them to apply own judgement in their work, can lead to positive changes in personality traits reflecting self-determination, such as the internal locus of control (Wu et al, 2015), proactive personality (Li et al, 2014), self-directedness (Kohn & Schooler, 1982) and self-competence (Gecas & Seff, 1989; Mortimer & Lorence, 1979). This is because stimulating jobs provide opportunities and challenges for employees, allowing them to effectively arrange their work activities to achieve better outcomes, and thus foster and strengthen a belief that they are able to control and master the external environment. Empirically, studies using a rigorous longitudinal design have reported that job autonomy is associated with an increase in internal locus of control (Wu et al, 2015) and proactive personality (Li et al, 2014). Wu (2016) also reported that an increase in job autonomy was directly associated with increases in agreeableness, conscientiousness and openness, and indirectly with an increase in extroversion and a decrease in neuroticism via changes in job stress. These findings suggest that an autonomous work environment can contribute to personality growth towards maturation, in the direction we discussed in Chapter 2.

Scholars have also suggested that demanding jobs can evoke stress-related experiences, and hence drive personality change in an undesirable direction, such as causing individuals to become more irritated emotionally and less ambitious motivationally (Kohn & Schooler, 1982; Sutin & Costa, 2010; Wu, 2016). However, results are not conclusive on this. In a two-wave longitudinal study over ten years, Sutin and Costa (2010) examined the cross-lagged associations between work characteristics (that is, decisional latitude, psychological demands, physical demands and hazardous work) and the Big Five personality traits. They found that hazardous work (exposure to dangerous work methods) in Year 1 was associated with a decrease in agreeableness, but they also found that greater psychological demands in Year 1 were associated with an increase in extraversion. In a three-wave longitudinal study, Li et al (2014) reported that high job demands in prior years were associated with growth in proactive personality over time. The findings on extraversion and proactive personality from these two studies suggest that job demands can push individuals to actively respond to such demands by attempting to master their environment, and thus that the impact of demands on personality change may not be as negative as we would expect. However, in another study, Wu (2016) used a large, nationally representative sample over a five-year period to examine whether changes in work characteristics (time demands and job autonomy) can drive changes in Big Five traits, especially changes in neuroticism and extraversion, via a stress–inducing mechanism. The study reported that over five years, an increase in time demands led to an increase in job stress over time, and the increase in job stress was associated with an increase in neuroticism and a decrease in extraversion. It is worth noting that findings from Sutin and Costa (2010) and Wu (2016) are not contradictory because these two studies examine different phenomena. While Sutin and Costa focused on how work characteristics (at Time 1) had lagged effects on personality change (during Time 1 and Time 2), Wu (2016) studied how the two changes (changes in work characteristics and changes in personality) were associated with each other during the study period. Nevertheless, more empirical evidence from properly designed longitudinal studies is needed to fully understand the role of job demands in shaping personality change.

Vocational characteristics

Vocational characteristics describe distinctive features that differentiate occupations. As indicated by Woods et al (2019, p 265), vocational characteristics 'describe work characteristics in ways that are not specific to individual jobs, but are rather representative of the environment at a higher level of abstraction capturing complex blends of tasks, goals, values, norms and behavioural expectations concerning a vocation'. While personality is usually considered an antecedent of individuals' vocational choice (Barrick et al, 2003; De Fruyt & Mervielde, 1999), such that people with certain personality traits are likely to choose specific occupations, recent studies have started investigating whether vocational characteristics can also drive personality change.

Using Hoekstra's (2011) six career roles (maker, expert, presenter, guide, inspirer, director), Wille et al (2012) investigated reciprocal relationships between individuals' Big

Five personality traits and their engagement in the six career roles over a 15-year period. They found that Big Five traits were associated with changes in career role engagement, and engaging in specific career roles was also associated with changes in specific personality traits. For example, engagement in the presenter role was associated with an increase in extraversion, engagement in the director and inspirer roles was associated with a decrease in agreeableness, engagement in the expert, guide, director and inspirer roles was associated with an increase in conscientiousness and engagement in the presenter, director and inspirer roles was associated with a decrease in neuroticism. The authors concluded that 'increases in career role engagement generally promote normative personality trait development' (Wille et al, 2012, p 318), that is, a normative decrease in neuroticism and a normative increase in conscientiousness over time, although not all findings come with straightforward interpretations.

In another study using the same cohort of participants, Wille and De Fruyt (2014) examined reciprocal relationships between Big Five personality traits and occupational characteristics based on Holland's taxonomy of occupations and interests (Holland, 1959). Holland's taxonomy describes six occupational environments (realistic, investigative, artistic, social, enterprising and conventional; RIASEC for short). The authors observed time-lagged effects of Big Five personality traits on occupational characteristics, and also observed time-lagged effects of occupational characteristics on Big Five personality traits. For instance, realistic characteristics predicted a decrease in neuroticism and an increase in agreeableness and conscientiousness, while enterprising and conventional characteristics predicted a decrease in openness to experience and agreeableness, and investigative characteristics predicted an increase in agreeableness. Again, while some effects were expected, others were not in line with expectations.

Also examining occupational characteristics, Helson et al (1995) examined women' occupational creativity and personality change. Based on participants' occupations, they assigned scores to indicate their level of occupational creativity, or 'the extent to which the women had spent their work lives in activity involving complex symbolic constructions, along with the degree of originality, energy, and success they had shown in this work' (Helson et al, 1995, p 1175). They then examined the association between occupational creativity and personality change and found that participants' occupational creativity was positively associated with changes in measures reflecting high levels of effective function, such as intellectual autonomy, ambition and openness. This finding suggests again that complex and challenging work can lead to personality growth.

In addition to studying specific vocational characteristics, the vocational and career pathways individuals take tend to impact their personality development. Lüdtke et al (2011) tracked about 2,000 German graduates from high school who either pursued university study or went into vocational training /work. They found that those choosing the latter (that is, a more vocationally oriented path) showed a greater increase in conscientiousness and a lesser increase in agreeableness than those entering universities, suggesting that career choice in the early stage has important implications for one's personality change. More recently, Li et al (2020) used two nationally representative samples (from the US and Australia) and found that upward career movement into leader positions was associated with an increase in conscientiousness, and that such a change could be explained by the increased role demand in leadership responsibilities.

A series of earlier studies have specifically looked into women's personality development as a result of their career choice, by partly taking into account the social roles these women chose to take (for example those of wife, mother or career woman). For instance, in the Mills study, which tracked 140 women who graduated from Mills College in 1958 or 1960, women who had been working over 20 years (from age 21 to

43) gained substantially in the 'independence' trait as compared to those who did not work during this time (Helson & Wink, 1992). The Radcliffe study included over 200 women from the Radcliffe College class of 1964, and tracked at least 100 of them at their mid-life stage and after retirement (Stewart & Vandewater, 1993). Using the data from this study, Newton and Stewart (2010) found that those who had worked during ages 28 to 43 showed stronger work or personal identity and less nurturing tendency compared to those pursuing family roles only. Roberts (1997) also found that women who work more and those who are more successful at work tend to become more agentic and norm adhering compared to their counterparts.

In terms of personality change for men specifically, Howard and Bray (1988) tracked 266 male managerial candidates at AT&T over 20 years, from their 20s to their 40s, to examine how their personalities changed over time. The 'ambition' factor in their personal preferences decreased steeply over the first eight years, possibly due to that participants gaining a more realistic view of the likelihood of promotion the company. These males increased in 'autonomy' – reflecting increased independence and decreased dependence on friendship during this time. Also interesting was participants' differences on the "nurturance" scale – those on the highest career track decreased in nurturance while those on the lowest career track increased in this dimension. The authors suggested this was due to executive responsibilities, which require individuals to focus more on the instrumental demands of the job rather than connecting with others emotionally. Somewhat consistently, Roberts et al (2003) reported that greater managerial power (or resource power) was associated with an increase in social potency (the quality of being forceful and decisive).

Finally, as we have briefly mentioned in Chapter 2, events in our key career stages can have implications for personality change. For example, entering the labour market for the first time (Specht et al, 2011) or starting a new job (Lüdtke et al, 2011) have been found to be associated with an increase in conscientiousness.

Contrarily, after retirement, people decrease their conscientiousness (Specht et al, 2011). These findings reflect the possibility that 'social roles force individuals to be more conscientious in times when they are integrated into the job market' (Specht et al, 2011, p 879). Broadly in line with this idea, Löckenhoff et al (2009) reported that after retirement, people become less fast-paced and vigorous (that is, they exhibit a decrease in the activity facet of trait extraversion), as well as less competitive and argumentative (that is, they exhibit an increase in the compliance facet of trait agreeableness), suggesting that after leaving the job market, people can become less active and more laid back.

Who do I work with? Work relations and personality change

Beyond what we do in our jobs, who we work with can also influence personality development. In this section, we discuss leaders (or supervisors), co-workers and organisations as the three main partners with which employees form important work relationships. These relationships can shape employees' work lives, and thereby their personality development.

Leaders (or supervisors)

Broadly speaking, leaders can influence followers via a structural process and a social influence process. The structural process involves, for example, how leaders assign and design tasks, construct the work environment and design the communication flow within and between teams. The previous section on work characteristics reflects one of the areas on which leaders can exert influence from this structural point of view. The social influence process involves leaders' influence on employees' beliefs and attitudes through interpersonal interactions, which are likely to shape employees' personality development. This is our focus in this section.

The social influence of leaders on employees has been well-recognised in research on leadership. For example, Shamir

(1991) proposed a self-concept-based theory of motivation, and argued that leaders can influence followers by shaping the way followers view themselves, which impacts how they engage in work behaviours. This idea was further elaborated by Lord et al (1999), who argued that leaders can influence and enact short-term changes in followers' self-perception, sense of their possible selves and goals, which then lead to enduring changes in their self-concepts.

Such an influence on followers' self-concepts is also specific-ally discussed in research on transformational leadership (Bass, 1990; Bass & Avolio, 1990). Transformational leadership is a leadership approach aimed at transforming followers' attitudes, beliefs, values and self-concepts (Shamir et al, 1993) in order to achieve performance beyond expectations. In contrast to transactional leaders, who view followers as an exchange party for contingent reward and who emphasise compliance for completing specific, well-defined performance, transform-ational leaders view followers as self-regulating agents who can regulate their motivation and behaviours based on their own attitudes and beliefs. As such, transformational leaders seek to influence their followers' attitudes and beliefs by showing a vision of the work unit or the organisation, stimulating thinking, and providing individualised support. Such a lead-ership style has been found to enhance followers' self-efficacy (Gong et al, 2009), their belief in their capability to perform actions to achieve specific goals, which acts as a key driver of self-regulation (Bandura, 1982, 1994). Transformational leadership can also shape followers' self-concepts in the long run via a Pygmalion mechanism, by enabling them to intern-alise leaders' expectations (Duan et al, 2017). For example, as transformational leaders encourage employees to challenge the status quo and build high self-efficacy, they can enhance followers' sense of agency and increase their proactive person-ality or openness over time.

As leaders vary in their leadership styles and behaviours, we expect that different leadership styles can drive followers' personality change in different directions. For example, authoritarian leaders may shape followers' personality change in an opposite direction compared to transformational leaders, as their tendency to stipulate rule-following behaviours can undermine their followers' proactive personality or trait openness. Authoritarian leaders also likely increase followers' neuroticism over time as followers may feel anxious about their performance and worry about any potential wrongdoing.

In addition to leadership styles, the relationship between leaders and followers, or the leader–member exchange (LMX) relationship (Graen & Uhl-Bien, 1995), can also play a role in followers' personality change processes. A leader can form LMX relationships of varying qualities with different followers, partly due to different levels of leader-follower schema fit (Epitropaki & Martin, 2005) or personality fit (Zhang et al, 2012). Followers that have higher-quality LMX relationships with their leaders are likely to gain more support and resources with which to do their work, which can help them cope better with job stress and strain – experiences that likely impact their trait neuroticism (Wu, 2016). These followers are also likely to be granted greater autonomy to decide what tasks to perform and when and how to do their jobs, a factor we have known to positively facilitate personality change in one's sense of agency and control. In addition, high-quality LMX relationships also likely deepen the influence of leadership styles on followers because followers may be more willing to internalise expectations and values from their leaders.

To our knowledge, whether or how leaders can shape followers' personality change has not been investigated empirically except for by Li et al (2014, 2019), which is surprising as leadership has been well recognised to influence employee development. In these two studies, the authors examined whether supervisor support can enhance employees' proactive personality or dispositional optimism, and did not find significant effect. As these are the only studies we know of having conducted such an examination, more studies are required to accumulate evidence. We believe followers' personality development should be considered under the scope of employee development, to identify how leaders can influence followers in a more enduring way.

Co-workers

Co-workers also play an important role in employees' work lives, and hence potentially impact their personality changes. Co-workers constitute an important part of the work environment that influences employees' behaviours, as people learn and regulate their behaviour by observing the behaviour of others (that is, through social learning) (Bandura, 1971). Specifically, employees observe what co-workers do and develop knowledge about the appropriateness of behaviours and form expectations about outcomes in their environment, and such observational learning especially occurs when people's observed targets (their co-workers for example) are perceived as similar to themselves (Schunk & Usher, 2012). This learning process can facilitate personality change via an Attraction-Selection-Attrition (ASA) mechanism (Schneider, 1987), through which employees become more similar to their co-workers (or else they leave the organisation). This is not to say that employees who stay can only converge in personality over time, as Roberts (2006) extended the ASA model into an ASTMA model, incorporating the possibility of personality change in two added stages: a transformation stage, which reflects how individuals' personalities can be transformed by work, and a manipulation stage, which reflects how individuals attempt to change their work. Roberts did recognise, however, that the ASTMA model predominantly addresses personality continuity rather that change, as most stages of this model (except for the transformation stage) describe individuals' conscious and unconscious effort to create 'a personal niche that reflects one's attributes' (Roberts, 2006, p 30).

Co-workers also act as important sources of social capital, on which employees can depend to cope when dealing with job demands or to achieve work goals, and which hence positively impact their performance and well-being (Bavik et al, 2020). As reported by Colbert et al (2016), positive work relationships with colleagues can contribute to task assistance, career advancement, emotional support, friendship, personal growth and opportunities to give to others. They found that these benefits can bring positive outcomes for employees in various respects, 'such that task assistance was most strongly associated with job satisfaction, giving to others was most strongly associated with meaningful work, friendship was most strongly associated with positive emotions at work, and personal growth was most strongly associated with life satisfaction' (Colbert et al, 2016, p 1199). In this regard, social support from co-workers can bring energy, meaning, and sense of confidence that is conducive to positive personality change. However, in the only two empirical studies that specifically examined co-worker support and personality change (Li et al, 2014, 2019), co-worker support did not seem to enhance employees' proactive personality or dispositional optimism. Again, like research on leadership, empirical research is sparse and more evidence is needed.

Organisations

Employees not only have relationships at the interpersonal level with their supervisors and co-workers, they also develop relationships with their organisations or employers. The employee-organisation relationship has been an interesting subject in management studies, and is mainly understood from a social exchange perspective such that employees and employers exchange obligations and promises to each other and establish psychological contracts (Coyle-Shapiro & Shore, 2007; Shore & Coyle-Shapiro, 2003; Shore et al, 2012). Organisations can offer support to employees to strengthen the employee-organisation relationship, and employees likely contribute more actively to organisations when they know they are cared for and protected by their employers (Eisenberger et al, 2001; Eisenberger et al, 1990; Eisenberger et al, 1986). Although psychological contracts and perceived organisational support have been widely studied, whether and how they could affect employees' personality development has not been examined.

However, the impact of employee–organisation relationships on employees' personality changes can be demonstrated by studies on the association between job insecurity and personality changes. Job insecurity, though usually understood as a job stressor, can also be understood as an indicator of the employee–organisation relationship. Job insecurity reflects one's 'concern about the future permanence of the job' (van Vuuren & Klandermans, 1990, p 133) and has been recognised as one of the facets in psychological contracts between employees and employers (Orvis et al, 2008; Rousseau, 1990; Turnley & Feldman, 1999). As job insecurity brings uncertainty, which can undermine the stability of one's life activities as well as one's ability to make long-term life plans, it can have negative implications for one's personality change. Two recent empirical studies confirm this. Li et al (2019) found that higher job insecurity was associated with decreased dispositional optimism for employees over time. Wu et al (2020) found that chronic job insecurity, or continuously experienced job insecurity over a long time period, was associated with an increase in neuroticism and a decrease in conscientiousness and agreeableness, the three traits relating to one's emotional, social and motivational stability and which are important for individuals' functional maturity (see Chapter 2). Importantly, Wu et al's study controlled for several other job characteristic factors (for example, job autonomy and time demands), thus demonstrating that job insecurity can be as important for personality development as are the factors representing what is involved in performing the job. In sum, employee–organisation relationships can be another important driver of personality change.

How am I doing? Work and career success and personality change

We now turn to evaluative experiences at work and how such experiences impact personality change. People like to know how well they are doing, and tend to regulate their actions and activities based on the feedback or evaluative experiences they have. When people receive positive feedback and evaluative experiences, they are likely to develop a positive view of themselves and a sense of self-determination, which helps drive personal growth. In line with this notion, several studies have found a positive effect of work and career success on personality change in relevant traits.

Job satisfaction, a general subjective appraisal of one's work experiences (Locke, 1969, 1976), has been associated with an increase in internal locus of control (Wu et al, 2015), a decrease in neuroticism and an increase in extraversion or communal and agentic positive emotionality (Roberts et al, 2003; Scollon & Diener, 2006). Growth in job satisfaction over time, as an indicator of career success trajectory, is also associated with an improvement in core self-evaluation, an overall self-perception that includes internal locus of control, trait neuroticism, self-efficacy and self-esteem (Wu & Griffin, 2012).

In addition to subjective perceptions, objective work and career success can lead to positive personality change. For example, Anderson (1977) reported that high firm performance enhances business owners' internal locus of control. Andrisani and Nestel (1976) reported that advancement in occupational status, advancement in annual earnings and re-entry into the labour force were related to an increase in internal locus of control. High income has been associated with an increase in dispositional optimism (Li et al, 2019) and a decrease in neuroticism (Sutin et al, 2009). Occupational prestige also tends to relate to reduced neuroticism (Sutin et al, 2009).

Two studies specifically focused on how upward job mobility affects personality change. Nieß and Zacher (2015) used propensity-score-matching techniques to divide employees who experienced upward job changes into managerial and professional positions versus those who did not, over a five-year span. They found that those who experienced upward job changes scored significantly higher in openness – but not in any of the other Big Five traits – than participants who did not. The authors suggested that this finding may be due to the fact that 'openness to experience is associated with intellectual ability and flexibility, divergent thinking, and the generation of new ideas, all of which seem to be especially important in managerial and professional position' (Nieß and Zacher, 2015, p 15). Wille et al examined the longitudinal reciprocal association between trait narcissism and upward mobility in managerial positions using data collected three times over 22 years. They found that the initial level of narcissism contributed to upward mobility, yet upward mobility in turn predicted a decrease rather than an increase in narcissism. They argued that such a finding may reflect a regulation of an optimal level of narcissism in management 'as extremely high levels of narcissism hinder rather than facilitate effective functioning in these roles, a phase of stabilisation rather than a continued increase of narcissism seems beneficial once individuals have reached a certain echelon in the hierarchy' (Wille et al, 2019, p 11).

Distal environment and personality change

Thus far, we have discussed work environment and work experiences as proximal drivers of personality change. We now turn to distal factors to discuss how the broader environment could also play a role in this regard.

Organisational environment

Factors at the organisation level, such as organisational struc-ture, organisational culture and organisational identity, could play a direct or indirect role in shaping employees' person-ality change. Organisational structure can influence, for example, the decision-making and information flow within organisations and the design of job responsibilities, which influence employees' experiences in performing their tasks and thus cause personality change. Tasselli et al (2018) discussed organisational pressure as one of the contextual factors that could have lasting impact on people's personality. In some of the extreme examples, they discussed how concentration camps, prisons and military settings, which impose total control on individuals, can adversely affect their personality functioning. We can infer from these examples that when organisations exert too much control over their employees, such as by imposing highly restrictive processes and policies that allow little room for individuals to make own decisions, they can negatively affect employees' personality development.

Organisational culture can also drive employees' personality change, via an ASTMA mechanism as we mentioned earlier. When employees find incongruence between themselves and their organisational culture, one way to resolve such person-environment misfit is to change their behaviours, attitudes or even values to be aligned with their organisations, which could lead to an enduring change in one's personality, especially if such demands persist (Harms et al, 2006; Woods et al, 2019).

Organisational identity is another factor that can change employees' self-perceptions and hence personalities. Organisational identity describes 'those features of an organisation that in the eyes of its members are central to the organisation's character or "self-image", make the organisation distinctive from other similar organisations, and are viewed as having continuity over time' (Gioia et al, 2013, p 125). While organisational identity can be understood from the social construction perspective, through which organisational identity is considered 'a self-referential concept defined by the members of an organization to articulate who they are as an organization to themselves as well as outsiders' (Gioia et al, 2013, pp 126–127), it can also be understood from the social actor perspective which is the perspective we adopt here. The social actor perspective 'emphasizes a view of organisations as entities making assertions about who they are as actors in society' (Gioia et al, 2013, p 127). From this perspective, we argue that organisational identity, constructed by organisations, may shape employees' self-concept via an organisational identification process (Ashforth & Mael, 1989). Although employees tend to identify with organisations with which they share similar values and attributes, employees can also identify with organisations that have different attributes and then change themselves into people who can represent these organisations (for example, employees may desire to enhance their self-esteem or social status by identifying with prestigious organisations). In addition, despite having general continuity, organisational identity can be malleable, as organisations adapt to changes in the environment by changing their business operations and key organisational characteristics. Such a change may trigger employees to reflect on how they identify with the new form of organisation, and a further process of self-identification and subsequent personality change could occur.

Societal environment

Societal factors such as social stratification have been discussed in studies on social structure and personality (see Spenner, 1988, for a review). Kohn and colleagues have conducted various studies along this line (Kohn, 1976, 1989; Kohn & Schooler, 1973, 1978, 1982; Kohn et al, 2000). The general theme of their examinations is based on the notion that an individual's standing in the social-stratification hierarchy can influence his/her work conditions, which in turn drive personality development in a specific direction.

Where does social structure enter into the picture? In all pertinent studies of the employed, including the study of employed Poles and Ukrainians under conditions of radical social change (Kohn et al, 1997), the uniform finding has been that position in the class structure and in the social-stratification hierarchy are highly correlated with the substantive complexity of people's work. Moreover, these facets of social structure affect personality largely because position in the class structure and in the social-stratification hierarchy are closely linked to the substantive complexity of work. Basic to this depiction is the crucial fact that the effects of the substantive complexity of work on personality are much the same throughout the social structure. (Kohn et al, 2000, p 201)

From the cultural perspective, societal culture can shape people's vocational choice, perception of work experiences and interpretation of career success, thereby driving personality development in specific directions. Societal culture also plays a significant part in personality change due to the fact that it 'shapes the types and qualities of roles afforded to individuals' (Roberts & Wood, 2006, p 18). As an example, gender role expectation continues evolving across generations, and in earlier periods fewer opportunities were afforded to women to express and realise their career preferences. In a study with women, Vandewater and Stewart (1997) contrasted women who began careers in the 1960s (a time in which it was unusual for women to have careers), those who began in the 1970s and '80s (a time that was much more supportive of women having careers), and women who never initiated careers. They found that those who began careers in the 1960s presented with midlife personalities of higher extraversion and assertiveness compared to those who never initiated careers, possibly due to the fact that they had to develop these personalities to survive in a male-dominated working environment. In contrast, those who began careers during the 1970s and '80s (who were in their 30s) demonstrated some characteristics of both extraversion and assertiveness as well as interpersonal warmth and connectedness. This may reflect the impact of a different, more supportive social/cultural context as compared to their counterparts in an earlier era. In general, people living in different historical and social periods can have different life trajectories due to the different social norms (Neugarten & Datan, 1973/1996), demonstrating how cultural and social change can drive personality development, partly by shaping people's vocational opportunities and work experiences. In a similar vein, we can expect different personality change trajectories for people living in different national cultural contexts.

International environment

Globalisation and technology changes render international contexts and dynamics increasingly relevant to our work lives. On the one hand, individuals are afforded more opportunities at a global level, as globalisation creates strong cross-border linkages and international mobility. International experiences can be a trigger of personality change as people are confronted with different values, beliefs and behavioural expectations when they live in unfamiliar cultures. In a study examining the impact of international mobility on personality change, Zimmermann and Neyer (2013) compared students who had short-term and long-term international mobility (or sojourners) with those who did not, over the course of an academic year. They found that those having international mobility showed increased trait openness, agreeableness and emotional stability, suggesting that international experiences can have positive influence on personality development. Bringing this to the work context, we are curious how expatriates could change their personality through overseas work experiences – an area that has not been specifically examined.

However, not all international mobility is as pleasant and voluntary as the kind sojourners likely have. International mobility resulting from civil wars or inter-country conflict can bring physical danger and psychological distress, as refugees confront radical changes in their living conditions and the need to fulfil basic survival requirements and to integrate themselves into a new society. How could refugees' personalities change as a result of such experiences? Empirical studies are extremely sparse in this area. We are only aware of a study which compared personality scores across a group of Swedish nationals, a group of Iranian refugees in Sweden and a group of Iranians living in Iran (Richter, Brändström, Emami & Ghazinour, 2004). The authors found that Iranian refugees in Sweden demonstrated personality profiles closer to those of the Swedish nationals than those living in Iran. This finding indicates that after resettlement in another culture, refugees may change their personality profile to deviate from their original culture and towards the new culture, suggesting personality change as result of potential culture adaptation. Nevertheless, we need more studies to understand how such an adaptation process functions, and whether work experiences in the resettled country can facilitate one's cultural adaption and personality development.

In addition to international mobility, global events can have a significant impact on how we work and live. During the time of writing, the coronavirus pandemic has hit almost all countries globally. Lockdown has been widely used as a measure to prevent the disease's spread. This has resulted in significant changes to our work, resulting in job losses, a sudden shift toward remote working and a lack of social support among others. How could a pandemic like this influence personality change? Job losses and heightened job insecurity, as has been previously discussed, can change personality in a negative way (Boyce et al, 2015; Li et al, 2019; Wu et al, 2020); even though involuntary job loss has been associated with an increase in openness, this seems to occur only for those individuals who are in better positions to secure new employment (Anger et al, 2017). The reliance on remote working, which represents a new form of work that has been unexpectedly imposed on many of us, may also impact our personality development. Such a practice may increase work–family interference, thus increasing stress and demands that negatively impact our personality. On the other hand, some individuals may experience enhanced job autonomy, which may have positive implications for personality development. In general, significant global events, such as the pandemic, can trigger drastic changes in the ways we work and live, and can change who we are – especially if their impact continues over a long period of time.

Summary

In this chapter we proposed a framework to depict how proximal work environment and distal social environment can shape personality (as well as be shaped by personality). We reviewed existing studies in the literature while highlighting the gap areas where further research is needed. In brief, empirical research so far has mainly focused on work and vocational characteristics and success. Numerous other broader organisational and social factors, which have important implications for one's work experiences, need to be investigated to understand their roles in individuals' personality changes. We will discuss these points in more details in Chapter 5.

FOUR

Intentional Personality Change: Individual Agency in Change and Interventions for Change

In Chapter 3, we reviewed studies that investigated how individuals' personality development is influenced by a wide range of external factors. These longitudinal studies primarily focused on personality change as a relatively passive process that requires a substantial length of time for such effects to occur. However, is there a possibility for personality change to be more actively facilitated within a shorter period, such as through purposefully designed interventions? While this idea may sound bold and potentially controversial from the personality psychology perspective (Mroczek, 2014), clinical psychology had long been operating under the assumption that personality, such as traits associated with depression and anxiety, can be changed through different intervention strategies (see Chapman et al, 2014, for a brief review).

The idea that personality change can be undertaken in a more active way is also in line with the agency perspective. It is not hard to understand that, as human beings, we are not merely 'pawns' of the environment and the demands life places upon us; instead, we can be active agents in initiating and driving our own personality change (McAdams & Olson, 2010; Denissen et al, 2013; Scarr & McCartney, 1983). An example of this can be seen in the vast amount of self-help books and training programmes available on the market, which have been suggested to be a $10 billion industry in the US alone (LaRosa, 2018). Indeed, self-pursued personality change is not only possible but desirable for many people who are motivated to improve themselves and willingly invest time, money and energy in doing so.

In this chapter, we will focus on how personality can be changed in a more active and intentional way, by discussing individuals' agency in this volitional change process and by understanding how interventions can be designed to facilitate such a change. The emerging nature of this area means that existing research specifically on interventions that change personality in work and vocational settings is very sparse. Therefore, we will draw evidence from the broader personality psychology literature, with the aim of providing insights for academics and practitioners working on personality change in the work and professional context.

Goals and desires for change

One of the most important factors leading to volitional personality change and growth can be individuals' motivation towards change. In line with the general motivational theory and goal-directed behaviour perspective (Ajzen, 1985), human behaviours are driven by intentions and goals. Goals depict personally desired end-states that one aspires to achieve (Kruglanski, 1996); strong, salient goals are likely to facilitate individuals' engagement in certain behaviours. The same is applied to personality change. For successful personality change to occur, individuals need to have goals and the motivation towards such a change. Recognising the importance of goals is also in line with the self-regulated personality development perspective (Denissen et al, 2013; Hennecke et al, 2014).

There is increasing research interest, therefore, in the goals individuals possess in relation to their personality change. Researchers have identified various innovative methods to unpack how goals of personality change can be measured. Some of them developed measures from existing Big Five frameworks to purposefully capture individuals' goals of changing each trait. Robinson et al (2015) employed a single item to describe the key adjectives associated with each trait, and asked participants whether they had a goal to be more, less or the same in each trait. Hudson and Roberts (2014) created a longer measure, by adapting an existing Big Five inventory to create a 'Change Goals Big Five Inventory', so that participants could report how they desired to change in relation to each of the Big Five items (for example, 'I want to be someone who … is considerate and kind to almost everyone'). Some other researchers took a more narrative approach. Baranski et al (2017, 2020) purposefully solicited participants' answers in relation to the aspects of their personalities that they desired to change, and then quantitatively coded these answers into Big Five traits. Miller et al (2019) attempted to investigate personality goals more situated in the general life domain. They asked participants to generate personal goals in life, and then coded responses to assess the extent to which such goals specifically represented goals of personality change (rather than other kinds of change). This approach puts personality change in a broad context, which helps to identify how prevalent personality change goals are compared to individuals' general life goals.

These innovative approaches enable us to directly capture individuals' personality change goals, and thus to understand to what extent people desire change. Results demonstrate that the majority of people want to change, and have goals of changing, at least some aspects of their personality. In several large-scale studies in the US, it was found that about 90 percent of participants wanted to become more extraverted, agreeable, conscientious and emotionally stable (Hudson & Fraley, 2016b; Hudson & Roberts, 2014). These are the traits reflective of the 'functional maturity' of personality development, which refers to the process of personality traits developing towards greater social desirability and adaptive functioning (Hogan & Roberts, 2004). Such evidence of the prevalence of change goals is replicated using different change-goal measures as was discussed previously (Baranski, 2018; Miller et al, 2019; Robinson et al, 2015). Furthermore, this observation has received support from studies comparing individuals in different age groups, showing that both younger and older individuals have desires for personality change (Hudson & Fraley, 2016b; Quintus et al, 2017), and it has received support in several cross-cultural studies, showing that the desire to change oneself is pervasive and universal in all populations around the world (Baranski, 2018; Robinson et al, 2015).

The trait that people most often want to change appears to be emotional stability (Hudson & Fraley, 2016b; Hudson & Roberts, 2014; Robinsons et al, 2015), and it is understandable that reducing one's neuroticism perhaps helps us more in terms of adapting to our life demands as compared to other traits. Regardless, the high percentages of change desires across almost all five key personality dimensions suggest that it is not just a small subset of the population – those who are less satisfied with their lives, for instance – who have the change desire; almost everyone wants to change something about themselves.

Such a phenomenon is not surprising, as the desire for a better self is a part of human nature. In fact, if we think of other highly related studies on self-concept, such as those focusing on 'possible selves' (Markus & Nurius, 1986), 'provisional selves' (Ibarra, 1999) or 'future work selves – which is about possible selves specifically in the work context – (Strauss et al, 2012), individuals' sense of self (that is, of who we are) can be flexible. It is a general human need to expand and grow ourselves, to bridge the gap between our current state and our desired state and increase our fit with our environment.

Interestingly, researchers have found that there is an inverse relation between individuals' goals of changing a particular personality trait and their current levels of that trait (Baranski et al, 2017, 2020; Hudson & Fraley, 2016b; Miller et al, 2019; Quintus et al, 2017). For instance, those who have goals of increasing their extraversion tend to have a lower current standing in extraversion. This suggests that individuals want to increase the traits in which they are currently lacking.

Do desires for change lead to actual change?

Having a motivation to change is important. But can having the desire or setting goals to change lead to actual change in personality? A series of studies produce somewhat mixed findings, but it appears reasonable to conclude that, while goals are useful, simply having goals does not guarantee change.

In a number of studies using both experimental design and field longitudinal design, Hudson and Fraley (2015, 2016a) tracked college students' personality traits and personality change goals multiple times throughout semesters that were up to 16 weeks long. They found that participants' change goals predicted their growth in the relevant personality traits; for instance, those having greater change goals in extraversion (either self-identified or induced by interventions) experienced greater change in this trait. They did notice, however, that the effect size of such change was stronger when participants received interventions to facilitate the change towards their goals, rather than being left alone to achieve goals by themselves. Recently, Hudson and colleagues (Hudson et al, 2020) conducted a mega-analysis (that is, an analysis aggregating participant-level data rather than study-level data) using 12 samples collected in their lab, all with similar designs despite using slightly different measures. Analysis on this large dataset replicated earlier findings. The traits for which change goals were most predictive of actual change appeared to be emotional stability and extraversion.

In contrast, several other studies cast some doubt on the predictive validity of personality change goals. Using a different measure than Hudson and colleagues, Robinson et al (2015) studied college graduates at two measurement points over a one-year span. They found that change goals did not show strong correlation with actual changes in personality traits. Interestingly, for traits such as emotional stability and conscientiousness, the desire to change actually reduced the standing in these traits. Baranski et al (2020) observed similar results in their study. Using two samples (a community sample and a college student sample), and with two different timespans (one year for the former, and six months for the latter), they found that volitional change desires did not predict actual change in general. They concurred with Robinson et al (2015) in that when changes did occur, they were in the opposite direction – the desires to increase extraversion, agreeableness and conscientiousness actually reduced participants' standing in those traits. Interestingly, they also found that participants perceived more change than the change that actually occurred, demonstrating some discrepancies between self-perceptions of change and the reality of change.

These contrasting findings are interesting. Possibly, the study designs impacted the results, as substantial variations exist in terms of the data collection frequency and duration and the measures used in these studies. In particular, Hudson and colleagues' series of studies involved assessing participants' personality change goals multiple times throughout the study period, while in studies by Robinson et al (2015) and Baranski et al (2020), participants were contacted only at the beginning and the end of the study. Therefore, the repeated and frequent contact in Hudson and colleagues' studies may have served as a 'reminder' to participants of their personality change goals, which may have played an important role in sustaining their trait change. Baranski et al (2020) suggested that, because personality change goals can often be cursory and frequently lead to less explicit outcomes, individuals may not put substantial efforts into these types of goals as compared to other, more concrete goals in life. Therefore, changing personality can be difficult if it is purely left to individuals' own devices, and some intervening sources are needed to sustain the efforts towards personality change. This point is reinforced by a recent study by Hudson et al (2019), which suggests that successfully changing personality traits indeed requires active and on-going commitment at a behavioural level, and that merely having the desire for change may not be sufficient.

Interventions that enable personality-trait-level change

As discussed, for personality change to occur, some levels of intervention appears necessary. In this section, we summarise findings from intervention-based studies in which personality change was facilitated. Understandably, most research in this area was conducted in the clinical psychology discipline, due to the long-standing interest of clinical psychologists in understanding how therapeutic interventions change important clinical outcomes, with personality traits such as anxiety and depression sometimes included. In contrast to this focus, there has been limited research on non-clinical populations (Bleidorn et al, 2019), and there has been even less focus on personality change interventions specifically in the work or professional context. Given that this book is aimed at understanding personality change at work, we only briefly comment on studies of the clinical context, and will put more emphasis on studies of the non-clinical context.

A systematic review and meta-analysis of research on how interventions change personality was recently conducted by Roberts et al (2017). They identified 207 studies, including studies in both clinical and non-clinical settings, that tracked personality change as a result of interventions. Their conclusion was that, collectively, these interventions led to marked changes in personality traits (d = .37 for the interventions which had an average of 24 weeks' duration). Though the majority of the studies included were clinically based, replicable findings were obtained from non-clinical interventions, demonstrating that effective personality change can occur for the general population. They also found that among the Big Five traits, emotional stability (first) and extraversion (second) demonstrated the largest changes as a result of interventions. Changes in agreeableness and conscientiousness were also statistically significant, while changes in openness were not. Overall, the positive and salient patterns of change in most of the Big Five traits demonstrate the efficacy of interventions in changing personality.

Despite the similar findings between clinical and non-clinical settings as reported in Roberts et al's (2017) review, clinical studies often involve clinically dominated strategies, such as using psychotherapies and pharmacological interventions, which are less applicable to the general population. Therefore, to provide meaningful insights as to how interventions in work and professional contexts can be designed to facilitate personality change, we discuss the several seminal studies conducted in non-clinical settings. We first report on the studies of the general population, and then discuss a small number of studies that were purposefully conducted in the professional context for working adults.

Hudson and colleagues conducted a series of studies in which they used self-directed goal-setting interventions among college students as a viable strategy for facilitating personality change. Hudson and Fraley (2015) asked participants to self-generate goals for personality change, and kept following up with them on these goals during a 16-week timespan. They found that when participants were asked to develop effective goals, that is, to develop concrete behavioural plans rather than vague, broad plans ('Call Andrew and ask him to lunch on Tuesday' rather than 'Be more sociable'), the intervention was effective and changes in conscientiousness, extraversion and neuroticism occurred. In an adapted version of this intervention, Hudson et al (2019) created challenges in relation to each of the Big Five traits (for example, a hypothetical challenge related to extraversion is to have a conversation with a stranger) for participants to take up when they set up their personality change goals. They then followed up with participants every following week to track whether they had completed those challenges. Their finding was that successful completion of these challenges led to positive growth in personality traits, especially in extraversion, conscientiousness and emotional stability. In contrast, simply accepting challenges but not completing them did not yield any effect.

Rather than leaving participants to self-develop goals and implement relevant strategies, some more active training interventions have been adopted. Jackson et al (2012a) conducted a 16-week training programme for old adults (aged from 60 to 94) aiming to improve cognitive ability, with the training focusing on inductive reasoning and complemented by puzzle exercises. They then assessed whether such training led to changes in the personality trait of openness to experience, in addition to changes in cognitive ability. Their results showed that the group receiving this training did report significant increase in the openness trait compared to the control group. In another study, Nelis et al (2011) designed an intervention study with the aim to improve the emotional competence of college students. The intervention was composed of an 18-hour training session (spread out over either two weeks or six weeks), complemented by a six-week email follow-up. Participants in the training group reported substantial improvement in emotional competence, and this improvement further led to a decrease in neuroticism and an increase in extraversion six months after the programme. In a more recent study, Stieger et al (2020) conducted a two-week smartphone-based intervention. They found that those who joined the self-discipline (a facet of conscientiousness) intervention showed greater increases in self-discipline, and those who joined the openness to action (a facet of openness to experience) intervention showed greater increases in openness to action. They also found the changes were maintained at two and six week follow-ups after the intervention.

Coaching as another viable intervention strategy for personality change has also been researched, as a number of studies examine the effectiveness of life coaching programmes. Using participants from a community sample, Spence and Grant (2005) conducted a ten-week coaching programme using both professional coaches and peer coaches, and examined the programme's impact on individual changes in a wide range of outcomes, with the Big Five personality included. In spite of the fact that the coaching was not targeted at personality change, the results showed that participants receiving coaching increased significantly in extraversion and openness to experience as compared to the control group. Martin et al (2014a) conducted a ten-week personality coaching programme, which was targeted at personality change in that the coaching focused on the personality facets that participants identified as the subjects of their change goals, and the coaching content focused on supporting changing those facets. They found that the coaching intervention resulted in significant progress in participants' identified personality change goals, while those in the control group did not demonstrate change. In a later reanalysis of the same data, Allan et al (2019) pointed out that across all participants, personality traits of conscientiousness, extraversion and neuroticism were changed as a result of this coaching. Moreover, changes in extraversion and neuroticism were maintained after three months.

It is also worth mentioning research conducted on meditation, which has been increasingly studied as a meaningful intervention for improving well-being. Some of this research included personality-trait change as one of the outcomes. Sedlmeier et al (2012) conducted a meta-analysis of the impact of meditation as an intervention strategy and identified studies in which personality was included. They identified 16 studies that measured neuroticism, and found that meditation intervention had a significant effect on reducing neuroticism ($r = .30$ for the correlation between group membership and dependent variables). The authors also identified nine studies that measured personality traits they categorised as 'negative personality traits' (egoism, dominance, etc.), and found that meditation also reduced standing in these negative traits ($r = .18$).

Finally, there are a small number of studies that specifically focused on personality change through interventions implemented in work and vocational settings. Krasner et al (2009) implemented a mindfulness programme with an eight-week intensive phase and a ten-month, less intensive maintenance phase for improving the well-being of primary care physicians. Though well-being was the main target of the programme, the authors included Big Five personality measures and found noticeable change in four out of the five traits after eight weeks. Moreover, positive changes in conscientiousness and emotional stability persisted after 15 months of the programme. In a recent study, Wang et al (2018) conducted a three-month training session aimed at improving a specific trait, goal orientation, in managers and professionals who were completing a part-time MBA programme. Goal orientation refers to individuals' tendencies in approaching achievement settings, as some people tend to focus on developing their knowledge and skills (a learning goal orientation), while others tend to focus on performance, either proving their competence (a performance-approach goal orientation) or avoiding negative judgment about their competence (a performance-avoidance goal orientation). This intervention study showed that through a purposefully designed personal development programme, with four sessions conducted over three months, effective change in goal orientation occurred towards a more optimal goal-orientation profile.

It is necessary to note that although studies of interventions targeting personality change at the trait-level are sparse in the work and vocational context, there are numerous training and development (T&D) programmes in organisations that are aimed at improving individuals' behaviours and/or leadership at work. This literature base is large and beyond the scope of this book, and thus we do not review it here. Although changing behaviours does not equal changing personality traits, behavioural change may be a precursor, and reflects state-level change, which ultimately leads to trait-level change. This point will be discussed in more detail in the next section.

Overall, existing intervention studies have provided promising findings for changing personality within a shorter time span. It should be noted that in most of the studies reported here, personality change was not the target of intervention, with only a few exceptions (Hudson & Fraley, 2015; Hudson et al, 2019; Martin et al, 2014a; Wang et al, 2018). Personality change effect has thus been considered as an 'accompanying effect' of the interventions (Allemand & Flückiger, 2017). This may suggest that if personality were the target of the interventions, an even stronger and larger effect size might be found.

Designing interventions that work: Understanding the process of change through a theory-driven approach

So far, we have provided evidence that interventions do work in changing personality traits, and that various intervention strategies can be adopted. However, in order to design effective interventions, we need to understand how personality change takes place through active interventions. This section thus reviews research evidence to provide a theoretical foundation for intervention design.

When it comes to interventions, many researchers have primarily discussed a bottom-up change process in which state-level changes are translated into trait-level change through repeated practices and the formation of habits (Chapman et al, 2014; Hudson & Fraley, 2015; Magidson et al, 2014; Roberts et al, 2006). The underlying principle of such a bottom-up process is similar to what we discussed in the previous chapter, in which state-level thoughts, feelings and behaviours are repeatedly elicited, either triggered by external factors or self-introduced; when this is sustained for an extended period of time, the entire density distribution of personality states can be shifted (Fleeson, 2001, 2004; Fleeson & Gallagher, 2009), leading to enduring changes at the trait level. Interventions are thus designed with the purpose of repeatedly eliciting and enacting day-to-day thoughts, feelings and behaviours, often through behavioural modification strategies (Hudson et al, 2019; Hudson & Fraley, 2015; Magidson et al, 2014).

Why is taking a bottom-up approach and targeting behavioural modification a viable strategy for changing personality traits? In a recently article, Allemand and Flückiger (2017) shed light on this issue. Drawing on the hierarchical structure of personality, they articulated that personality is not only understood as including broad, general, less malleable traits, but is also reflected in medium-level constructs (for example, habits) and narrow constructs (states) which are more situationally dependent and thus changeable. Such a conceptualisation indicates that, while it is possible to target interventions directly at trait-level constructs, the relative endurability and stability of traits means that interventions at this level are not only costly but need to be very powerful to change individuals' systemic patterns of thoughts and behaviours, and hence that they are less feasible. Interventions that change lower-level constructs (at the state level) are more feasible, yet they may suffer from the lack of transferability into changes at the trait level. Therefore, interventions targeted at changing habits (medium-level constructs) through repeated practice and reinforcement of states may be the most feasible for rendering permanent change at the trait level.

It is necessary to note, however, that while bottom-up processes have been the focus of studies and appear fruitful in guiding personality change interventions, some level of consideration has also been given to the top-down approach, despite only a few (for example, Allemand & Flückiger, 2017) explicitly recognised as doing so. As we will discuss in more detail later in the chapter, the various frameworks researchers have put forward all point to the necessity of understanding participants'/clients' values and beliefs – despite these being higher-order constructs that are less changeable – as these factors are important in guiding and sustaining individuals' motivations to change. We will discuss a number of theoretical frameworks that have been recently proposed, with the aim of showing that these frameworks can be used as guiding principles in designing personality change interventions.

Magidson et al (2014) applied behavioural activation, as informed by expectancy-value theory (EVT) (Eccles, 2009), to illustrate how personality traits can be changed through interventions. EVT highlights the importance of *value* and *expectancy*, arguing that when individuals place high value on a task, and expect to succeed at it, they will develop ambitious goals and persist in achieving these goals. The application of behavioural activation therefore is aimed at facilitating engagement in goal-related behaviours that are considered important, enjoyable and in line with individuals' values. With this approach, individuals are encouraged to monitor their daily activities and behaviours, explore their values and identify goals in line with those values, as well as to develop plans and see them through. Using an illustrative case study, Madison et al demonstrated how a substance-dependent individual was assisted to change conscientiousness, a trait that is particularly relevant to goal setting and goal achievement. Although this paper focused on conscientiousness, the underlying principles of the goal-directed and self-regulated process appear applicable to changing other personality traits.

Hennecke et al (2014) proposed a framework for self-regulated personality development. This framework is built on the underlying assumption that individuals play an active role in changing their personality and employ self-regulatory mechanisms to achieve the goal of changing their personality. In this framework, the authors delineated three key conditions that need to be met to facilitate self-regulated personality change. First, individuals must perceive the new trait-related behaviours as desirable and necessary. Second, individuals must consider themselves as being capable of performing the new trait-related behaviours; that is, the desired change is feasible. Third, individuals need to frequently enact and practice trait-relevant behaviours over time, so that these behaviours become habitual, and eventually achieve a stable shift in personality traits. While the first and second conditions delineate the goals and motivations individuals need to possess, the third condition concerns the process through which initial change goals are translated into actual change. Like gaining other competencies or skills, gaining changes in personality traits requires purposeful practice and repetition of trait-relevant behaviours so that the behaviours become automatic. This conceptual model is useful for highlighting the key areas interventions need to address in order for effective personality change to occur.

More concrete practices facilitating personality change have been discussed in the coaching literature. By interviewing coaches and psychologists, Martin et al (2014b) developed a stepwise process that offers practical guidelines for coaches to adopt in facilitating personality change. A key part of this process involved goal setting – that is, understanding the current self and identifying the gaps between the current self and the ideal self; these gaps serve as the foundation for developing personality change goals and developing actionable coaching plans. The ongoing coaching sessions then focused on implementing these plans, reviewing progress towards goals and maintaining the change. In general, the coaching process needs to develop clients' self-awareness, appropriately manage their motivations, take into account their confidence in their ability to change and facilitate sustained efforts towards that change (Rollnick et al, 1999). These factors are well in line with what has been proposed by Hennecke et al (2014).

Inspired by research models adopted in psychotherapy, Allemand and Flückiger (2017) outlined several key factors for designing personality change interventions for the non-clinical population. They articulated four general mechanisms for change: 1) actuating discrepancy awareness, which enables individuals to actuate the costs and benefits of their standing in a personality trait, such as by understanding the discrepancy between their current state and their desired state relative to that trait; 2) activating strengths and resources, which is about activating clients' individual capabilities and strengths to enable change; this uses a strength-based approach to create and maintain a positive feedback loop and foster individuals' openness towards change; 3) targeting beliefs, expectations and motives to realise insight, which describes a reflective process in which clients are facilitated to become aware of their motivational determinants (for example, their unconscious goals and beliefs), so as to develop new insights; 4) practicing targeted behaviours, which focuses on concrete behaviours and actions, so that new behaviours are learned, reinforced and acquired. The authors highlighted that to realise effective outcomes, all four areas need to be achieved, as has been shown in psychotherapy studies. In discussing their model, Allemand and Flückiger specifically highlighted that while some of these factors (factor 4, and to some extent factor 1) are primarily about state-level interventions (hence a bottom-up process), other factors, such as factor 3, are aimed at changing constructs at the more broad and abstract level (beliefs and values, hence representing a top-down process). They suggested that incorporating both processes enables more holistic and sustainable personality development.

There is remarkable commonality among these theoretical frameworks. They all highlight the importance of *motivation* as the fundamental driver of change, a point we made earlier in the chapter. The slight difference lies in that Martin et al (2014b) and Allemand and Flückiger (2017) articulated more specifically that it is the discrepancy between the current self and the ideal self that creates the motivation – echoing the key condition outlined by Boyatzis (2006) in his intentional change theory. All of these frameworks also highlight the importance of creating *expectancy* – that is, participants' belief that change can happen. Strategies to increase such belief include drawing on their existing capabilities and instilling confidence. Finally, all of them discuss purposeful *practice*, supported by regular reviews and reflections, as an important mechanism through which change can be sustained. Overall, these models provide useful guidelines for intervention designers as well as for individuals themselves embarking on the journey of personality change.

Other considerations in personality change interventions

How soon does personality change occur?

We have articulated several key factors, or ingredients, that interventions need to have in order to facilitate personality change. Another important question in intervention design concerns duration; that is, how long the intervention needs to be for effective personality change to occur?

In our review of studies earlier in the chapter, it can be seen that most studies were of intervention programmes ranging from eight weeks to 16 weeks in duration – that is, between two and four months (Hudson & Fraley, 2015; Hudson et al, 2019; Jackson et al, 2012a; Martin et al, 2014a; Nelis et al, 2011; Spence & Grant, 2005; Wang et al, 2018). Krasner et al's (2009) intervention was longer than others in that they included a 'maintenance phase' of ten months, though the initial intensive training lasted for eight weeks, which was within the same timespan as other studies. Stieger et al's (2020) smartphone-based intervention was an exception, being of only two weeks' duration, although the intensity of this intervention needs to be noted, as it involves daily activities.

Roberts et al's (2017) meta-analysis provided more sum-mative findings on this, by evaluating the effect size and duration of interventions across studies. Their conclusion is that interventions can have a substantial effect on personality change in the first eight weeks; beyond eight weeks, longer interventions did not seem to induce greater effect size. However, interventions can not be too short as well, as those shorter than four weeks yielded small effects.

Such findings are very encouraging, as they challenge the assumptions that personality is changed mostly in a passive way and that it takes a long time to occur, and show that personality change through well-designed and implemented interventions may only require between two to three months of dedicated effort. From an organisational point of view, this duration is in line with many of the training programmes typically implemented in workplaces. This gives confidence to organisational psychologists and human resource professionals to design effective interventions to facilitate personality change. However, it is also important to point out that the aforementioned intervention studies have rarely examined the sustainability of change beyond the intervention, thus it remains an open question 'how change sticks' after initial successful change in traits. We thus need more research that effectively follows up and tracks individuals over time, beyond the scope of the interventions, to provide more informative evidence in this regard.

Individual variation in change

It is necessary to recognise that in understanding how interventions change personality, we are likely to overlook the fact that not all individuals change in the same way, as group data on change often mask critical individual differences in change (Pervin, 1994). Indeed, longitudinal studies on passive personality change have provided evidence for interindividual differences in intra-individual change, as some people remain stable while others change; and individuals also differ in the rate of change (Mroczek & Spiro, 2003). This indicates that individuals are also likely to respond differently to interventions that target personality change.

In an earlier part of this chapter we discussed the importance of motivation, and people can indeed differ in their motivation. For instance, some evidence has pointed out that individuals who lack certain traits tend to have a stronger desire to change that trait (Baranski et al, 2017, 2020; Hudson & Fraley, 2016b; Miller et al, 2019). Those who are less satisfied with their lives may also have a stronger motivation for change, in the hope that changing personality could improve some aspects of their lives (their relationships, health, well-being and functioning in society) (Heatherton & Nichols, 1994; Hudson & Robert, 2014; Quintus et al, 2017). Additionally, even though having goals is important, those motivated by intrinsic goals rather than extrinsic goals are more likely to effectively develop their personality (Hudson & Fraley, 2017).

People may also differ in their ability to enact and sustain change. One indicator of this ability can be individuals' attachment styles. In a recent empirical study, Wang et al (2018) found that those with an avoidant attachment style, identified by a defensive style in social relationships, demonstrated less personality change in trait-level goal orientations; those with an anxious attachment style, identified by anxiety and fear of social relationships, relied on facilitator support and only changed when they perceived a high level of support from facilitators. The authors suggested that because personality change involves navigating a new territory of 'self' and can be challenging, those with an avoidant attachment style may be 'walling off' change, while those with an anxious style depend on having a 'secure haven' such as is provided by facilitators who can support them through their journey. Another factor related to this ability may be individuals' beliefs in change, as those with a strong belief that personality is fixed (sometimes called 'entity orientation') (Dweck, 2008) may be less likely to believe they are able to change their personality (Allemand & Flückiger, 2017; Hudson & Fraley, 2017). Indeed, in a non-intervention-based study of personality change, it was found that those with less strong entity orientation increased in four out of the Big Five traits (Robins et al, 2005). A further factor could be self-monitoring, which Tasselli et al (2018) discussed in a conceptual paper, arguing that self-monitoring reflects a flexible self-presentation that is attuned to and easily changed by situations, though it is unclear whether a flexible personality pattern as demonstrated by high self-monitoring can effectively translate into long-term, permanent change in personality. Related to this, others mention personality strength (Dalal et al, 2015) as another potentially relevant factor, as those with strong personalities may exhibit little change over time.

Individual difference in personality change has generally been a neglected area (Mroczek et al 2006; Tasselli et al, 2018), and a lot more research is needed to understand such nuance and complexity in more depth.

Other contextual enablers of change

Even though intervention itself has a very strong and powerful contextual influence on personality change, it is likely that other contextual factors can play an important role in facilitating such a change, both during and beyond the intervention. For instance, social support, which has been often discussed as important in facilitating behavioural change (Clifford et al, 1991), may be a contextual factor worth considering. By helping individuals sustain self-esteem, providing feedback and information and reinforcing their efforts, the support provided by significant others can encourage individuals throughout their efforts to change and can provide a buffer for strains associated with challenging experiences. Studies based on the self-determination theory, for instance, have repeatedly highlighted the importance of support from others, especially the type of support that protects and sustains individuals' autonomy in their personal development and change journey (Lynch et al, 2011; Ryan & Deci, 2008).

Studies on personality change interventions have shown that, beyond the intervention's curriculum design, support from programme facilitators is an important predictor of change, though such support may be more important for some individuals than others, as we reported in the above section (Wang et al, 2018). Other studies of the coaching context also showed the importance of support from either professional coaches or peer coaches (Martin et al, 2014a, 2014b; Spence & Grant, 2005) in enabling individuals to follow through a process towards personality change. Although research that specifically focuses on personality change as outcome is sparse, we can draw insights from the clinical psychology literature (Ackerman & Hilsenroth, 2003), which suggest that the characteristics and style of the key support person (the therapist, for example) play an important role in intervention outcomes. Overall, there is still a lot we need to learn about the other contextual factors that need to be in place in order for personality change to take place more effectively, either through interventions or through the volitional personality change process.

Summary

We started this chapter by highlighting that personality change can occur through a self-regulated and goal-oriented process such that effective change needs to start with a strong desire for, and intention to, change that originates from oneself. However, a growing line of research also demonstrates that while having such intentions is important, merely desiring change may not be sufficient, as active and purposeful efforts are needed to change individuals' thoughts, feelings and behaviours in order to realise trait growth.

We reviewed evidence from existing intervention studies in which personality-trait-level changes were reported. Our focus was on studies conducted in non-clinical settings so as to provide evidence that is more directly applicable to organisations and managers. Our review demonstrates that personality change can be meaningfully achieved through interventions, despite the fact that many such interventions are not targeted at changing personality. We then discussed several theoretical perspectives to provide insights on why and how such change could occur, with the aim to provide more concrete guidelines for practitioners who are interested in designing and implementing interventions to facilitate positive personality growth.

Finally, we discussed a number of other considerations in intervention-based personality change studies. We summarised evidence to provide guidelines on how long the interventions need to be for change to occur. We also discussed individual differences in change, and contextual factors that support change. Needless to say, as this field is still in its infancy, a lot more research is needed to shed light on these interesting questions.

While this chapter focuses on intervention strategies created and designed by others, it is important to highlight that a powerful agent of change ultimately resides in oneself. Even without interventions, some people naturally take steps to change their personality traits; for instance, those who desire to have higher extraversion may intentionally engage in more extraverted behaviours, such as networking and socialising, in an attempt to change this trait. Also, for interventions to take effect, it is down to individuals to put in the effort and actively participate as required (Chapman et al, 2014; Denisson et al, 2013). We did not specifically distinguish self-introduced interventions in this chapter, as we believe many of the same principles can be applied when individuals take a purely self-directed approach to changing their personality.

FIVE

Implications of Personality Change at Work for Research and Practice

We have discussed in detail the interactive relationship between work and personality change, and articulated how personality change can occur both as a result of multilevel influences from global, national and organisational contexts, and as a result of one's deliberate and intentional efforts, with and without external intervening forces. By this time, we have established that personality change does occur at work, through both passive and active influences, and that such change can have important implications in our work and lives in general.

In this final chapter, we will move beyond the review of existing evidence and point out the implications of personality change studies for future research and practice. First, we will draw on existing evidence to identify unresolved debates and understudied areas in personality change research, and provide suggestions for future research. We will also comment on methodological issues in studying personality change, providing a brief overview of the existing and future approaches for continuing research in this area. We will then address the practical implications for society, organisations and for employees themselves. By doing so, we hope to shed light on how organisations, leaders and individuals can take on board the dynamic perspective toward personality to adapt their thinking and practices within and beyond organisations.

Implications for future research: conceptual advancement

In this section, we summarise and discuss what we know and what we should further explore to understand work and personality development. We firstly address issues relating to the scope of personality traits and the scope of work experiences, and then indicate other topics for exploration.

The scope of personality traits

The majority of research efforts so far have focused on the Big Five traits. The advantage of such a dedicated focus is that it helps us to integrate research evidence under a consistently applied framework and thus provides a common language for communicating about the phenomenon of personality change. However, moving beyond this focus can present unique opportunities for expanding our knowledge on important, specific personality factors that are subject to change.

As a few examples that we have discussed earlier, scholars have examined how proactive personality (Li et al, 2014) and personality trait optimism (Li et al, 2019) can be changed by both the employment characteristics (job insecurity for example) and relational characteristics of work (for instance, social support), and how core self-evaluation can be changed by perceptions of work success (job satisfaction for example) (Wu & Griffin, 2012). These studies have important implications as they highlight how positive individual attributes (instead of more neutrally oriented attributes such as those described in the Big Five model) can be shaped and facilitated by work contexts, and may thus have more important implications for leaders, organisations and societies in developing employees' positive personality traits and enabling them to possess more psychological capitals that are conducive to success and well-being (Luthans et al, 2007). On the other hand, studies focusing on the dark side of personality appear to be particularly scarce in the personality change literature. A recent study filled this gap, by demonstrating how climbing the corporate ladder and achieving career success can increase the narcissistic personality trait (Wille et al, 2019). Studies like this are important for understanding not just how the work environment shapes the development of positive, highly desired traits, but also how it can unintentionally facilitate the growth of traits that may harm individuals, groups and societies.

Another approach worth considering is to move beyond studying each trait as independent, isolated dimensions and instead integrate them through a person–centred approach. Individuals' personalities are not simply an aggregate of individual traits but are also reflected in the compositional structure of these traits (Asendorpf, 2015). Therefore, personality consistency and change should involve the understanding of this holistic personality configuration. Such change in personality profiles over time has been much less studied (see Damian et al, 2019; Specht et al, 2014b for a few exceptions who studied personality-profile change in the general life domain). This will be an interesting and important research question for understanding how the work and occupational context drives personality change.

The scope of work experiences

As we discussed in Chapter 3, a substantial amount of research effort has been put into understanding how one's job, its task and vocational characteristics, shapes personality change. In contrast, much less has been studied in relation to broader social- and organisational-level factors. The same observation has been made by Woods et al (2019), who reinforced the importance of study this missing link in how group-level factors impact personality change. Drawing on the person–environment fit perspective, they found that substantial efforts have been focused on person–job fit, but much less on person-organisation fit. We have also indicated that organisational, societal and international environment can play a distal role in shaping one's work experiences and thus one's personality change. Compared to studies on work and vocational characteristics, research on the role of organisational, societal and international environment in personality development needs further development.

In addition to the consideration of different environmental factors, the focus on objective, acute events or subjective, chronic environment is another angle to consider. Although both types of experiences can drive personality change, personality psychologists and organisational psychologists have assigned them different weights in terms of their focus. Personality psychologists tends to focus more on how objective, acute events, such as the start of new relationships and careers, divorce and widowhood, can impact personality (see Bleidorn et al, 2018 for a review), while organisational psychologists tend to focus on how subjective, chronic environment, such as perceptions about one's job characteristics and career experiences, can change one's personality (see Woods et al, 2019 for a review).

We believe that each focus comes with unique strengths and limitations, and that thus a more integrated approach at both the conceptual and empirical levels would help advance our knowledge of personality change at work. Life event studies focus on objective status change – that is, how individuals transit from one status to another (Bleidorn et al, 2018). This approach avoids running into perceptual biases associated with using self-reported subjective perceptions, as individuals can adjust their perceptions of the environment to be congruent with their personality (Harms et al, 2006). However, the reliance on life event analysis can also mask the real impact of these events, as sometimes even though the objective environment might be different, individuals can enact similar roles so as to promote the consistency of their personality. As discussed in relation to the 'role continuity principle' by Roberts and Wood (2006, p 25), 'This coherence of social roles transcends the physical environment that facilitates personality consistency over time'. This means that, for instance, even though individuals may enact a job change (that is, a life event), the nature of their roles may remain similar. On the other hand, profound change in environment can also occur without making significant change in status (Denisson et al, 2014); for instance, individuals can craft their jobs so as to have different characteristics ('job crafting') (Wrzesniewski & Dutton, 2001) without necessarily enacting job changes. Additionally, in many cases, life event analysis tends to focus on a short-term effect, as status transition represents a one-off event, thus studies like this may be limited in unpacking the long-term effect of environmental factors, while studies using subjective perceptions of environment can more effectively tease out the reciprocal effect between environment and personality (for example, Wille et al, 2019). In sum, we need evidence from both perspectives in order to understand how personality change occurs as a result of the environment.

A good example of this can be seen by contrasting the study by Boyce et al (2015) and the study by Wu et al (2020). Boyce et al studied how the objective life event of unemployment, and the duration of unemployment, impacted personality change, while Wu et al studied how perception of job insecurity, and the duration of such perception, impacted personality change. The relevance of the external conditions that individuals are exposed to in these two studies makes it highly useful to integrate them and compare the findings. It seems that both the objective loss of one's job and the subjective experience of feeling worried about the potential risk of losing one's job have a negative impact on personality change, especially in terms of reducing agreeableness and conscientiousness. There is a slight difference in regard to other traits, in that unemployment tends to reduce openness, while the subjective perception of job insecurity tends to reduce emotional stability. A possible explanation, as hinted at by Wu et al, is that unemployment is a negative status that people are certain of, while the perception of insecurity represents an uncertain condition, and thereby heightens emotional arousal and increases personality neuroticism. Overall, as shown in this example, pulling evidence together from studies of objective life events and of subjective perceptions of relevant external conditions enables us to triangulate the evidence and generate a more complete picture about how these conditions change personality.

Cross-cultural similarities and differences in personality change

As a new field, research on personality change is still primarily conducted in Western, developed countries, especially in the US and Europe. Among a few exceptions, Bleidorn et al (2013), in a web-based study, reached out to young adults across 62 countries, including many emerging economies in Asia and South America, and revealed a cultural effect on personality change such that personality differences in these countries were associated with cultural differences in the normative timing of adult role transitions. Robinson et al (2015) investigated whether goals to volitionally change one's personality differed across Iran, China and the UK, and suggested that, while there were cultural similarities, and neuroticism was the trait that participants in all countries desired to change (that is, to reduce), there were also cultural differences such that Iranian participants' personality change goals were more socially desirable. In another study, Baranski (2018) approached participants from across 58 countries to understand the similarities and differences across cultures in terms of volitional personality change. They found that the majority of participants across the world demonstrated intentions for volitional personality change (VPC), yet large cultural variations emerged; for instance, less than 30 percent of participants from Israel demonstrated

VPC, while over 80 percent of participants from Indonesia demonstrated VPC. These cross-cultural studies, though highly important, were largely based on cross-sectional data, and many relied on student samples.

Overall, cross-cultural studies are very limited in the personality change literature (Bleidorn, 2015; Caspi et al, 2005). This limits the generalisability of the findings. Longitudinal studies from different countries are needed, especially from those non-Western countries that have different social norms, studies of which are extremely sparse at the moment. A possible avenue is to engage in cross-cultural studies using archival data collected from different countries. Though such methods have limitations (a point discussed later in the methodological section), they at least provide longitudinal datasets that allows personality change to be properly captured over time. Cross-cultural comparative studies like this would allow us to unpack how cultural factors can act as powerful macro-environmental drivers of personality change, as well as how they can be meaningful moderators for the relationship between other antecedents and personality change (Bleidorn, 2015).

Understanding the outcomes of personality change

By shifting the paradigm of treating personality as an outcome rather than an antecedent, research has moved on substantially in challenging a previously set assumption that personality is stable and in unlocking exciting new research agendas regarding personal change and development. However, this doesn't mean that the traditional approach in examining how personality predicts outcomes is unimportant.

Scholars have suggested that personality change involves change both in identity (how we see ourselves), and in reputation (how others see us) (Roberts, 2006; Tasselli et al, 2018). However, more long-term outcomes can also occur such that new behaviours, work performance, income, well-being, health and interpersonal relationships are likely affected as a result of such personality change. The new personalities people adopt may also suggest that a previously fitting role may no longer fit, thus new experiences may be sought after. The impact of personality change on important outcomes should be expected given years' of research on the importance of personality traits in our work and life, including work performance (Barrick & Mount, 1991; Hurtz & Donovan, 2000; Tett et al, 1991), leadership capabilities (Bono & Judge, 2004; Judge et al, 2002a), occupational status (Damian et al, 2017), income (Denissen et al, 2018), subjective well-being (Diener & Lucas, 1999; Steel et al, 2008), and even longevity (Mroczek & Spiro, 2007; Roberts et al, 2007).

There is emerging evidence pointing to how personality change is associated with changes in various outcomes across life domains, including mental and physical health, job attainment and satisfaction, and interpersonal relationships, among others (see Bleidorn et al, 2019, for a review). However, it should be noted that many of these existing studies are based on correlational results, such that changes in personality and changes in outcomes were collected during the same time period, thus causality is yet to be ascertained. More rigorous study designs are needed, such as collecting multiple measurements over a long time span so that the antecedents of personality change can be temporally separated from the outcomes of personality change, or using experimental/quasi-experimental methods to include control groups (Bleidorn, 2015; Bleidorn et al, 2019) in disentangling the causality between personality change and resulting consequences.

Implications for future research: methodological advancement

Studying the change phenomenon is a challenging endeavour in terms of study design, data collection and as data analytics. Therefore, substantial consideration should be given to the methodological front in investigating personality change. Here we briefly discuss some of these considerations while alluding to future research directions.

Moving beyond self-reported change

Personality change is most often assessed by self-reporting as participants complete personality measures on each measurement occasion. Apparently, this is the most feasible data-collection approach given the long-term efforts required for data collection. However, the limitations of this method need to be recognised, as self-reporting is retrospective and thus less time sensitive (Roberts, 2018), and it can reflect an 'illusion of change' (Specht et al, 2014a, p 226) that distorts the real change effect. In general, self-reported change provides only 'a rather narrow window into personality change processes' (Bleidorn et al, 2019, p 19).

Rather than over-relying on self-reporting, many researchers advocate for a more diverse, multi-method strategy to assess personality, such as using behavioural observations, others' reporting, physiological measures, or implicit tests (Bleidorn et al, 2018; Caspi et al, 2005; Geukes et al, 2017; Specht et al, 2014a; Wrzus & Mehl, 2015). Researchers also advocate for more sensitive measurements, such as experience-sampling or event-sampling designs (Wrzus & Roberts, 2017) which, despite still being self-reported, can illuminate short-term change processes and distinguish trait-level change from state-level change (Bleidorn et al, 2018). This latter point is important; as Roberts (2018) recently illustrated, there are different change systems underpinning personality change, including state-level fluctuations, a 'pliable' system that reflects permanent modification to seemingly fixed phenotypes, and an 'elastic' system that reflects changes in phenotypes but only for a certain period of time rather than permanently. Therefore, we need a wide range of short-term and long-term personality measurements to disentangle which proportions of the measures are attributed to each of these different change systems. Needless to say, such efforts are costly, and researchers may thus need to be more creative in securing large and ongoing funding to conduct such research. A recently published study (Quintus et al, 2020) provided an example of how such a multi-method approach can be achieved.

Study design: measurement occasions and study duration

To effectively capture the change phenomenon of personality and to understand how it occurs as a result of work context, we need to track both personality and contextual factors over time through multiple measurement occasions. This has not always been achieved in work and personality change studies, some of which tend to capture personality measures at two time points but contextual factors at only one time point, often at or close to the time point of the second personality measure (for example, Roberts et al, 2003; Le et al, 2014). However, studies – especially those conducted more recently – tend to employ a proper cross-lagged design, with measurements of both personality and work-related factors collected at multiple time points (Hudson et al, 2012; Li et al, 2014, 2019; Roberts, 1997; Sutin & Costa, 2010; Wille et al, 2012, 2019; Wille & De Fruyt, 2014; Wu, 2016; Wu & Griffin, 2012; Wu et al, 2015, 2020). It is important to highlight that only the latter type of study, which represents true longitudinal design, can yield accurate findings about the relationship between person-ality change and work (Woods et al, 2013). Ideally, we need studies that include multiple measurement occasions rather than relying on only two waves of data collection – such a design is limited in unpacking change trajectory, investigating non-linear effect, validating continuity and change patterns, and examining directionality in the reciprocal effects (Caspi et al, 2005; Woods et al, 2013).

In terms of study design in relation to the duration of data collection, the majority of longitudinal studies have been designed assuming that personality change occurs only in a rather slow manner. For instance, the aforementioned prominent studies in the work and personality change literature tend to typically cover a timespan ranging from four to ten years (with a few spanning over 20 years), often using panel data that were collected at the regional or national level. These data have substantial advantages in providing large, representative samples that span over a long time period, thus presenting unique opportunities to study personality change. They also have limitations, however, in that they were not designed to assess personality change, and thus the personality variables were often collected too infrequently or the collections were too widely spaced (Bleidorn et al, 2019). For instance, in the German Socioeconomic Panel Study and the Household, Income and Labour Dynamics in Australia Survey, which many research studies were based on, personality was assessed only every four years. When measurement of personality takes place in such an infrequent manner, it is impossible to tie personality change to a specific transitional event (Luhmann et al, 2014).

Moreover, such a data-collection interval may be too long to effectively capture personality change. While the exact timescale required for personality change to occur remains unknown, there is evidence that personality change can happen more quickly; for instance, studies have shown that 12 months is sufficient to enact personality change as triggered by major life events such as graduating (Bleidorn, 2012) or moving overseas (Zimmermann & Neyer, 2013). There is also evidence that when interventions are used to purposefully induce personality change, meaningful change can take place within just a few months (see Roberts et al, 2017 for a review). We thus need studies that use multiple and more frequent assessments that are sensitive enough to provide 'sufficiently high temporal resolution' (Bleidorn et al, 2019, p 22). These high-resolution studies can also provide meaningful data that help to unpack the process of personality change, such as by identifying meaningful mediators of change, an area that is still largely underinvestigated (Geukes et al, 2017; Roberts & Nickel, 2017).

Effect size of change

The magnitude of the personality change we should be expecting is worthy of consideration, as it is reasonable to expect that there is still substantial stability in personality and thus that the magnitude of change may not be large. Studies focusing on mean-level change, for instance, have suggested that when we focus on the really long-term span, such as across one's life, change can actually be rather significant. For instance, in terms of mean-level change across lifespan, many traits demonstrated changes close to one standard deviation, which is a large effect size in psychology (Roberts et al, 2006; Roberts & Mroczek, 2008). When personality change is facilitated via active interventions (therapies for example), it seems that just a few weeks' intervention can result in half a standard deviation of change in personality traits (Roberts et al, 2017).

When considering how personality change is shaped by external environment and life experiences, it seems that such an effect is generally small to modest. Studies on life event analysis have demonstrated that the effect size of most objective life events on personality change sits within .20 (see Bleidorn et al, 2018 for a review). In the work domain, researchers have focused on how subjective perception of work experiences (rather than objective events) impacts personality change. As we mentioned, there is large variation in study design, and only those designs with multiple measurement occasions for both personality variables and work-related variables can provide an accurate estimation of the lagged effect of work experience on personality change. Across these studies, especially studies where standardised coefficients were reported, effect sizes that were found statistically significant ranged from .04 to .17 for job characteristics such as job autonomy and job demand (see Wu et al, 2020, for a brief review). When broader work experiences are considered, such as individuals' experiences that reflect their work success (for example, occupational attainment and power) and social investment in their job (job involvement for instance), slightly larger effect sizes are found, and can reach the .20 range (Hudson et al, 2012; Robert et al, 2003) or occasionally even .30 (Hudson & Roberts, 2016) – although substantial differences in effect size existed depending on the measures being used for capturing personality as well as work experiences. Overall, these effect sizes appear small to modest at most.

Despite the very modest effect size in these studies, it is important to recognise that these effects are still meaningful and important. As indicated by Adachi and Willoughby, small effects are meaningful because they reflect 'an ongoing process of cumulative effects and thus may have a substantial impact on the outcome over time' (Adachi & Willoughby, 2015, p 119). Indeed, even modest changes in personality can have profound consequences for individuals' lives (Roberts et al, 2008).

Implications for policy and practice

The fact that individuals' personalities are malleable, and can be meaningfully modified and redirected by life and work experiences, has substantial implications for policy, practices as well as individuals' daily lives. Although this idea may not be new in other domains (for instance, educational and developmental psychology have been concerned with developing children's attributes such as self-regulation, self-esteem, curiosity and integrity, and clinical psychology is aimed at reducing individual tendencies toward attributes such as anxiety and depression to improve human functioning and well-being), the fact that personality change can occur more broadly across life domains and across life stages means that it has far-reaching implications for every single one of us. In particular, as we spend such a significant amount of time at work during our adulthood, the accumulating evidence that work experiences and work events can change our personality highlights the critical role of work in producing long-lasting impact on individuals. In the following section we discuss the implications of personality change for individuals, organisations and society.

What does personality change mean for individual employees?

As individuals we need to let go of the determinist view of personality and to understand that personality can be meaningfully changed by our life experiences, and that work can play a substantial role in this change. The career path we choose, the jobs and tasks we take on, the leaders and co-workers we socialise with and the various systematic and random events and experiences we go through at work can all shape who we turn out to be. It is important to be aware of the long-term consequences of work for ourselves, as work not only affects our performance and well-being – the consequences that people mostly think about – but can also leave a more permanent mark on our personality. For instance, if we have been chronically exposed to poorly designed jobs that deprive us of our autonomy and that provide little opportunity to apply our knowledge and skills, we can end up feeling less in control of our lives in general (Wu et al, 2015), consequently creating a negative spiral. Therefore, we need to be cautious in choosing the tasks, jobs and careers we engage in, and constantly reflect on how we have changed as a result of these experiences. As sometimes we can lose insight and awareness after being exposed to certain environments for a long time, it is also useful to seek feedback from important others, such as partners, friends, or mentors, to solicit their observations on our personality change as a result of our work.

More importantly, we need to take on board the idea that while work does change us, we can also be active agents of our own personality change. This self-directed journey starts from a clear goal about what aspects of our personality we intend to change. We also need to plan and develop specific strategies for working towards this change. Different strategies can be adopted, such as changing behaviours (for instance, being more active in getting to know new people and building a social network) or changing cognition (for example, paying more attention to how one interprets certain events and responds emotionally) (Baranski et al, 2017). But perhaps most importantly, we need to commit to ongoing and persistent effort for change to be enacted and maintained. As found by researchers (Hudson et al, 2019), simply having a goal to change or desiring change is insufficient for change to occur. Our current standing in personality traits is deeply ingrained, and change is extremely difficult – think of how difficult it is to quit smoking or drinking. Therefore, very strong self-regulation is required over a reasonably long time so that individuals can move beyond a short-term 'bump' in personality and create a more permanent change. Ultimately, it rests in our own hand to drive and sustain meaningful personality change.

How can organisations apply the concept of personality change?

The recognition that personality change can occur at work highlights the important role organisations can play in facilitating positive personality development, and it also offers new insights into how we plan and implement various personnel policies and practices.

Recalibrating personnel-selection practices to incorporate the personality change concept

Current personnel-selection practices have largely been based on the fixed perspective on personality such that job candidates are selected based on how their personality profiles fit with what is required in the job; and once hired, they are expected to continue behaving in line with what their personality profiles suggest. However, this understanding needs to be revised given what we have learned about personality change.

First, while recognising that congruence between personality and job demands may be beneficial for individuals and organisations (Woods et al, 2013, 2019), we should not rule out the possibility that individuals can develop their personality traits to bridge incongruence. Some individuals may actually appreciate the challenge (rather than seeing it as a stressor) presented by incongruence, and thrive on this challenge. As we discussed in Chapter 4, if they have the desire and goal towards personality change, and willingly put in continuous efforts to enact change, these individuals may eventually turn out to be better fitting and more valuable employees for organisations, due to their high learning orientation and learning ability. Certainly, this adds another layer of complexity for personnel selection practitioners, requiring they be more innovative in their selection strategies to allow candidates like these to be considered.

Second, given the changing nature of personality, it is important to put a timestamp on the personality testing being administered during selection, so that hiring managers are aware that this test reflects only a snapshot of individuals' personalities at that particular point in time, and that such a profile will be likely to change once this person is in the job. Although we do not yet know exactly how long such a profile will remain valid, as the rate and direction of personality change is dependent on individuals' unique experiences at work, the evidence that meaningful personality change could happen within 12 months if significant events occur (Bleidorn, 2012; Zimmermann & Neyer, 2013) may indicate that we should use caution in relying on personality-testing profiles that are older than 12 months.

Designing jobs to facilitate personality growth

As we discussed in Chapter 3, although the idea that work shapes who we are is not a new concept, empirical evidence that provides broad support for such an idea is only accumulating in recent years. The empirical evidence, especially evidence of the association between work characteristics and personality change, thus suggests that work design can be a factor in facilitating positive personality change while preventing negative change. A direct piece of evidence on this point is from Wu (2016), who showed that increasing job autonomy and decreasing time demands can lead to a decrease in job stress, and thereby an increase in extraversion and a decrease in neuroticism. This finding directly suggests that changes in work characteristics can lead to changes in personality.

There are many ways that jobs can be redesigned to facilitate positive personality change. In addition to job autonomy, increasing job complexity can broaden one's exposure to different tasks and build different skills and competence. In the long run, through mechanisms such as the broaden-and-build mechanism (Fredrickson, 2001), these jobs could enhance individuals' self-efficacy and enable them to become more agentic. Enhancing task significance via a relational job design (Grant, 2007) could also drive personality change. For instance, by enabling individuals to directly see the impact of their work on beneficiaries, individuals could develop a strong prosocial motivation and possibly increase in trait agreeableness. While job design is traditionally considered from a top-down perspective (that is, employees' jobs are designed by managers or organisations), recent research on job crafting (see Zhang & Parker, 2019, for a review) indicates that employees can be proactive in this and design their jobs using a bottom-up approach. Job crafting can thus be a useful approach for employees, especially those who like to change their personality in a specific way, to self-direct their personality development journey. As such, in addition to designing better jobs for employees, organisations can also consider how to offer opportunities and supports that empower employees to craft their jobs.

Expanding the focus of training and development to include personality change

T&D is critical in enhancing human capital within organisations. However, organisations' T&D focus has been mainly on imparting knowledge, skills, and competencies that enable employees to work effectively. Although there is increasing incorporation of personal development in leadership development programmes, there is still not an explicit recognition that personality change and growth could be part of this focus. As is well articulated by Bleidorn et al (2019), although focusing on immediate change is easier, such change may only comprise short-lived adaptations. Ultimately, it is to organisations' benefit to help employees achieve more permanent changes that 'stick' over time, which is in line with the focus of training transfer literature (Baldwin & Ford, 1988). More broadly, as individuals spend such a significant amount of their time at work, organisations have a social responsibility to facilitate meaningful and holistic personal growth rather than simply focusing on providing work-related knowledge and skills – a point has been well highlighted in the humanistic perspective on human resource development (Chalofsky et al, 2014).

As we have discussed in Chapter 4, theoretical advancement in the personality change literature over recent years means that human resource developers are now equipped with more theories and evidence with which to design interventions that work. Although facilitating personality change through interventions is still in its infancy, several theoretical frameworks (Hennecke et al, 2014; Madgidson et al, 2014; Martin et al, 2014b) have been developed to shed light on the key factors and considerations in intervention design. We recommend practitioners consider such existing practices and identify innovative ways to apply the personality change theories in practice, and collect evidence that can further enrich these theories.

Highlighting personality change in career development

Similar to what we discussed in the personnel selection section, the idea that the concept of person–job fit needs to be revised to take into account personality change also has broad implications for career and vocational development. As pointed out by Woods et al (2013, 2019), employees can be encouraged to engage in a career that they would like, despite the fact that it may be less consistent with their existing personality. In this regard, coaching, mentoring and career counselling can focus on probing into areas of personality-job incongruence to identify how personality change can be enacted to bridge this incongruence, rather than only considering jobs or areas of jobs as the main target of change. For those individuals who do not experience personality-job incongruence, aspects of the personality change literature, such as the corresponsive principle we discussed in Chapter 2, can also be useful, as they help individuals to understand how their existing personality can be deepened and consolidated by their work experiences.

Coaches, mentors and counsellors can take on board the idea that personality can change actively, and facilitate self-directed personality change journeys in their clients. It is important for coaches, mentors and counsellors to convey such a belief to their clients and to provide substantial support for individuals' autonomy when doing so, as personality change involves stretching outside ones' comfort zone and can thus be a risky and uncertain journey (Wang et al, 2018). Certainly, self-directed personality change primarily involves efforts by oneself, a point we mentioned previously.

How can society embrace personality change?

The fact that personality can change, and change meaning-fully, as a result of work experiences, as well as experiences in other life domains, can shift public perception of the fixedness of personality in adulthood, and offers important insights for fostering a growth mindset among all individuals (Dweck, 2008). An understanding and acceptance that personality can be changed in adulthood is an empowering thought that can encourage all individuals to pursue this change and make their lives better. The evidence for personality change also indicates that interventions can be meaningfully employed to assist in this endeavour so that personality growth towards greater social and psychological maturity can be facilitated (Bleidorn et al, 2019). Educational systems such as business schools can also more actively consider how personality development can be part of the core focus of education. Indeed, it has been recognised that business education tends to overly focus on 'knowing' (facts, frameworks and theories) and not sufficiently on 'doing' (the development of skills and capabilities), and certainly very little on 'being' (being who we are and developing deep insights into our strengths and weaknesses) (Datar et al, 2010). Therefore, educational institutions have the collective responsibility to pay more attention to personal development, which in a way reconnects with the core purpose of education; that is, to focus not only on imparting knowledge but also on developing human potential – a focus that is clearly visible in children's education but which seems to be significantly missed in adult learning. In Chapter 4 we discussed an example programme that was designed to facilitate development in individuals' trait-level goal orientation through an elective course in an MBA programme, and demonstrated that such change was not only possible but also positive (Wang et al, 2018). We call for a more explicit focus like this in our educational system, and for a more dedicated effort to empirically track personality change as a result of education.

Concluding remarks

Personality is not set in stone, and can be shaped both by the broader social and economic context as well as by what we do in our day-to-day work and by the decisions we make for ourselves. More importantly, personality change can be actively facilitated, either by ourselves or external forces. We hope the evidence discussed in this book can provide all individuals with the confidence that they are able to adopt new personalities as long as they try. There is no reason to settle for a fixed belief about 'who we are', and to shy away from taking on one's most critical life tasks – changing oneself for the better, so that we can lead a happier, more successful and more rewarding life.

People may start with different temperaments and different aptitudes, but it is clear that experience, training and personal effort take them the rest of the way. (Dweck, 2008, p 5)

References

Ackerman, S. J. & Hilsenroth, M. J. (2003) 'A review of therapist characteristics and techniques positively impacting the therapeutic alliance', *Clinical Psychology Review*, 23(1): 1–33.

Adachi, P. & Willoughby, T. (2015) 'Interpreting effect sizes when controlling for stability effects in longitudinal autoregressive models: Implications for psychological science', *European Journal of Developmental Psychology*, 12: 116–28.

Ajzen, I. (1985) 'From intentions to actions: A theory of planned behavior', in J. Kuhl & J. Beckman (eds) *Action-control: From Cognition to Behavior* (pp 11–39), Heidelberg: Springer.

Alarcon, G., Eschleman, K. J. & Bowling, N. A. (2009) 'Relationships between personality variables and burnout: A meta-analysis', *Work & Stress*, 23(3): 244–63.

Allan, J., Leeson, P., De Fruyt, F. & Martin, S. (2019) 'Application of a 10 week coaching programme designed to facilitate volitional personality change: Overall effects on personality and the impact of targeting', *International Journal of Evidence Based Coaching and Mentoring*, 16(1): 80–94.

Allemand, M. & Flückiger, C. (2017) 'Changing personality traits: Some considerations from psychotherapy process–outcome research for intervention efforts on intentional personality change', *Journal of Psychotherapy Integration*, 27(4): 476–94.

Allport, G. W. (1937) *Personality: A Psychological Interpretation*. New York: Holt.

Allport, G. W. (1961) *Pattern and Growth in Personality*. New York: Holt, Rinehart & Winston.

Allport, G. W. & Odbert, H. S. (1936) 'Trait-names: A psycho-lexical study' *Psychological Monographs*, 47(1): i–171.

Anderson, C. R. (1977) 'Locus of control, coping behaviors, and performance in a stress setting: A longitudinal study', *Journal of Applied Psychology*, 62(4): 446–51.

Andrisani, P. J. & Nestel, G. (1976) 'Internal-external control as contributor to and outcome of work experience', *Journal of Applied Psychology*, 61(2): 156–65.

Anger, S., Camehl, G. & Peter, F. (2017) 'Involuntary job loss and changes in personality traits', *Journal of Economic Psychology*, 60: 71–91.

Asendorpf, J. B. (2015) 'Person-centered approaches to personality', In M. L. Cooper & R. Larsen (eds), APA *Handbook of personality processes and individual differences,* Washington, DC: American Psychological Association.

Ashforth, B. E. & Mael, F. (1989) 'Social identity theory and the organization', *Academy of Management Review*, 14(1): 20–39.

Ashton, M. C. & Lee, K. (2007) 'Empirical, theoretical, and practical advantages of the HEXACO model of personality structure', *Personality and Social Psychology Review*, 11(2): 150–66.

Ashton, M. C. & Lee, K. (2019) 'How well do Big Five measures capture HEXACO scale variance?', *Journal of Personality Assessment*, 101(6): 567–73.

Ashton, M. C., Lee, K. & Goldberg, L. R. (2004a) 'A hierarchical analysis of 1,710 English personality-descriptive adjectives', *Journal of Personality and Social Psychology*, 87(5): 707–21.

Ashton, M. C., Lee, K., Perugini, M., Szarota, P., de Vries, R. E., Di Blas, L., Boies, K. & De Raad, B. (2004b) 'A six-factor structure of personality-descriptive adjectives: Solutions from psycholexical studies in seven languages', *Journal of Personality and Social Psychology*, 86(2): 356–66.

Ashton, M. C., Lee, K. & de Vries, R. (2014) 'The HEXACO Honesty-Humility, Agreeableness, and Emotionality Factors: A Review of Research and Theory', *Personality and Social Psychology Review*, 18(2):139–52.

Baldwin, T. T. & Ford, J. K. (1988) 'Transfer of training: A review and directions for future research', *Personnel Psychology*, 41(1): 63–105.

Baltes, P. B. (1997) 'On the incomplete architecture of human ontogeny: Selection, optimization, and compensation as foundation of developmental theory', *American Psychologist*, 52(4): 366–80.

Bandura, A. (1971) *Social Learning Theory*, New York: General Learning Press.

Bandura, A. (1982) 'Self-efficacy mechanism in human agency', *American Psychologist*, 37(2): 122–47.

Bandura, A. (1994) 'Self-efficacy', in V. S. Ramachaudran (ed), *Encyclopedia of human behaviour* (Vol 4, pp 71–81), New York: Academic Press.

Bandura, A. (2001) 'Social cognitive theory: An agentic perspective', *Annual Review of Psychology*, 52(1): 1–26.

Baranski, E. N. (2018) *Volitional Personality Change across 58 Countries*, Riverside, CA: University of California Riverside.

Baranski, E. N., Morse, P. J. & Dunlop, W. L. (2017) 'Lay conceptions of volitional personality change: From strategies pursued to stories told', *Journal of Personality*, 85(3): 285–99.

Baranski, E. N., Gray, J., Morse, P. & Dunlop, W. (2020) 'From desire to development? A multi-sample, idiographic examination of volitional personality change', *Journal of Research in Personality*, 85.

Barrick, M. R. & Mount, M. K. (1991) 'The big five personality dimensions and job performance: A meta-analysis', *Personnel Psychology*, 44(1): 1–27.

Barrick, M. R. & Ryan, A. M. (2003) *Personality and Work: Reconsidering the Role of Personality in Organizations*, San Francisco, CA: John Wiley & Sons.

Barrick, M. R., Mount, M. K. & Judge, T. A. (2001) 'Personality and performance at the beginning of the new millennium: What do we know and where do we go next?', *International Journal of Selection and Assessment*, 9(1/2): 9–30.

Barrick, M. R., Mount, M. K. & Gupta, R. (2003) 'Meta-analysis of the relationship between the Five-Factor Model of personality and Holland's occupational types', *Personnel Psychology*, 56(1): 45–74.

Bartram, D. (2005) 'The great eight competencies: A criterion-centric approach to validation', *Journal of Applied Psychology*, 50(6): 1185–203.

Bartram, D. & Guest, F. (2013) 'Incorporating personality assessments into talent management processes', in N. Christiansen & R. P. Tett (ed), *Handbook of Personality at Work*, Abingdon: Routledge.

Bass, B. M. (1990) 'From transactional to transformational leadership: Learning to share the vision', *Organizational Dynamics*, 18(3): 19–31.

Bass, B. M. & Avolio, B. J. (1990) 'The implications of transactional and transformational leadership for individual, team, organizational development', *Research in Organizational Change and Development*, 4: 231–72.

Bateman, T. S. & Crant, J. M. (1993) 'The proactive component of organizational behavior: A measure and correlates', *Journal of Organizational Behavior*, 14(2): 103–18.

Bavik, M. Y. L., Shaw, P. J. D. & Wang, D. X. H. (2020) 'Social support: Multi-disciplinary review, synthesis, and future agenda', *Academy of Management Annals*, 14(2), 726–58.

Bell, S. T. (2007) 'Deep-level composition variables as predictors of team performance', *Journal of Applied Psychology*, 92(3): 595–615.

Benet, V. & Waller, N. G. (1995) 'The Big Seven factor model of personality description: Evidence for its cross-cultural generality in a Spanish sample', *Journal of Personality and Social Psychology*, 69(4): 701–18.

Berry, C. M., Ones, D. S. & Sackett, P. R. (2007) 'Interpersonal deviance, organizational deviance, and their common correlates: A review and meta-analysis', *Journal of Applied Psychology*, 92(2): 410–24.

Bleidorn, W. (2012) 'Hitting the road to adulthood: Short-term personality development during a major life transition', *Personality and Social Psychology Bulletin*, 38(12): 1594–608.

Bleidorn, W. (2015) 'What accounts for personality maturation in early adulthood?', *Current Directions in Psychological Sciences*, 24(3): 245–52.

Bleidorn, W., Klimstra, T. A., Denissen, J. J., Rentfrow, P. J., Potter, J. & Gosling, S. D. (2013) 'Personality maturation around the world: A cross-cultural examination of social-investment theory', *Psychological Science*, 24(12): 2530–40.

Bleidorn, W., Buyukcan-Tetik, A., Schwaba, T., Van Scheppingen, M. A., Denissen, J. J. & Finkenauer, C. (2016) 'Stability and change in self-esteem during the transition to parenthood', *Social Psychological and Personality Science*, 7(6): 560–69.

Bleidorn, W., Hopwood, C. J. & Lucas, R. E. (2018) 'Life Events and Personality Trait Change', *Journal of Personality*, 86(1): 83–96.

Bleidorn, W., Hill, P. L., Back, M. D., Denissen, J. J. A., Hennecke, M., Hopwood, C. J. et al (2019) 'The policy relevance of personality traits', *American Psychologist*, 74(9): 1056–67.

Bono, J. E. & Judge, T. A. (2003) 'Core self-evaluations: a review of the trait and its role in job satisfaction and job performance', *European Journal of Personality*, 17(S1): S5–S18.

Bono, J. E. & Judge, T. A. (2004) 'Personality and Transformational and Transactional Leadership: A Meta-Analysis', *Journal of Applied Psychology*, 89(5): 901–10.

Bono, J. E. & Vey, M. A. (2007) 'Personality and emotional performance: extraversion, neuroticism, and self-monitoring', *Journal of Occupational Health Psychology*, 12(2): 177–92.

Borghuis, J., Denissen, J. J. A., Oberski, D., Sijtsma, K., Meeus, W. H. J., Branje, S. & Bleidorn, W. (2017) 'Big Five personality stability, change, and codevelopment across adolescence and early adulthood', *Journal of Personality and Social Psychology*, 113(4): 641–57.

Bouchard, T. J. & Loehlin, J. C. (2001) 'Genes, evolution, and personality', *Behavior Genetics*, 31(3): 243–73.

Boyatzis, R. E. (2006) 'An overview of intentional change from a complexity perspective', *Journal of Management Development*, 25(7): 607–23.

Boyce, C. J., Wood, A. M., Daly, M. & Sedikides, C. (2015) 'Personality change following unemployment', *Journal of Applied Psychology*, 100(4): 991–1011.

Brousseau, K. R. (1978) 'Personality and job experience', *Organizational Behavior and Human Performance*, 22(2): 235–52.

Brousseau, K. R. (1983) 'Toward a dynamic model of job-person relationships: Findings, research questions, and implications for work system design', *Academy of Management Review*, 8(1): 33–45.

Brousseau, K. R. & Prince, J. B. (1981) 'Job-person dynamics: An extension of longitudinal research', *Journal of Applied Psychology*, 66(1): 59–62.

Campbell, W. K., Hoffman, B. J., Campbell, S. M. & Marchisio, G. (2011) 'Narcissism in organizational contexts', *Human Resource Management Review*, 21(4): 268–84.

Caspi, A., Roberts, B. W. & Shiner, R. L. (2005) 'Personality development: Stability and change', *Annual Review of Psychology*, 56(1): 453–484.

Cattell, R. B. (1943) 'The description of personality: basic traits resolved into clusters', *The Journal of Abnormal and Social Psychology*, 38(4): 476–506.

Cattell, R. B. (1945) 'The description of personality: principles and findings in a factor analysis', *The American Journal of Psychology*, 58(1): 69–90.

Chalofsky, N. E., Rocco, T. S. & Morris, M. L. (eds) (2014) *Handbook of Human Resource Development*, Hoboken, NJ: John Wiley & Son.

Chamorro-Premuzic, T. (2011) *Personality and individual* differences (2nd Ed), London: BPS Blackwell.

Chapman, B. P., Hampson, S. & Clarkin, J. (2014) 'Personality-informed interventions for healthy aging: Conclusions from a National Institute on Aging work group', *Developmental Psychology*, 50(5): 1426–41.

Chiaburu, D. S., Oh, I.-S., Berry, C. M., Li, N. & Gardner, R. G. (2011) 'The five-factor model of personality traits and organizational citizenship behaviors: A meta-analysis', *Journal of Applied Psychology*, 96(6): 1140–66.

Church, A. T., Katigbak, M. S. & Reyes, J. A. S. (1998) 'Further exploration of Filipino personality structure using the lexical approach: do the big-five or big-seven dimensions emerge?', *European Journal of Personality*, 12(4): 249–69.

CIPD (2017) Resourcing and talent planning survey report.

Clausen, J. A. & Gilens, M. (1990) 'Personality and labor force participation across the life course: A longitudinal study of women's careers', *Sociological Forum*, 5(4): 595–618.

Clifford, A., Tan, S. Y. & Gorsuch, R. (1991) 'Efficacy of a self-directed behavioral health change program: Weight, body composition, cardiovascular fitness, blood pressure, health risk, and psychosocial mediating variables', *Journal of Behavioral Medicine*, 14(3): 303–23.

Cloninger, S. (2009) 'Conceptual issues in personality theory', In P. J. Corr & G. Matthews (eds), *The Cambridge Handbook of Personality Psychology* (pp 3–26), Cambridge: Cambridge University Press.

Colbert, A. E., Bono, J. E. & Purvanova, R. K. (2016) 'Flourishing via workplace relationships: Moving beyond instrumental support', *Academy of Management Journal*, 59(4): 1199–223.

Connolly, J. J. & Viswesvaran, C. (2004) 'The role of affectivity in job satisfaction: A meta-analysis', *Personality and Individual Differences*, 29(2): 265–81.

Costa, P. T. & McCrae, R. R. (1995) 'Domains and facets: Hierarchical personality assessment using the Revised NEO Personality Inventory', *Journal of Personality Assessment*, 64(1): 21–50.

Coyle-Shapiro, J. A. M. & Shore, L. M. (2007) 'The employee-organization relationship: where do we go from here?', *Human Resource Management Review*, 17: 166–79.

Dalal, R. S., Meyer, R. D., Bradshaw, R. P., Green, J. P., Kelly, E. D. & Zhu, M. (2015) 'Personality strength and situational influences on behavior: A conceptual review and research agenda', *Journal of Management*, 41(1): 261–87.

Damian, R. I., Spengler, M. & Roberts, B. W. (2017) 'Whose Job Will Be Taken Over by a Computer? The Role of Personality in Predicting Job Computerizability over the Lifespan', *European Journal of Personality*, 31(3): 291–310.

Damian, R. I., Spengler, M., Sutu, A. & Roberts, B. W. (2019) 'Sixteen going on sixty-six: A longitudinal study of personality stability and change across 50 years', *Journal of Personality and Social Psychology*, 117(3): 674–695.

Datar, S., Garvin, D. A. & Cullen, P. G. (2010) *Rethinking the MBA: Business Education at a Crossroads*, Boston: Harvard Business School Press.

De Fruyt, F. & Mervielde, I. (1999) 'RIASEC types and big five traits as predictors of employment status and nature of employment', *Personnel Psychology*, 52(3): 701–27.

De Fruyt, F., Bartels, M., Van Leeuwen, K. G., De Clercq, B., Decuyper, M. & Mervielde, I. (2006) 'Five types of personality continuity in childhood and adolescence', *Journal of Personality and Social Psychology*, 91(3): 538–52.

Demerouti, E., Bakker, A. B., Nachreiner, F. & Schaufeli, W. B. (2001) 'The job demands-resources model of burnout', *Journal of Applied Psychology*, 86(3): 499–512.

Denissen, J. J. A., van Aken, M. A. G., Penke, L. & Wood, D. (2013) 'Self-regulation underlies temperament and personality: An integrative developmental framework', *Child Development Perspectives*, 7(4): 255–60.

Denissen, J. J. A., Ulferts, H., Lüdtke, O., Muck, P. M. & Gerstorf, D. (2014) 'Longitudinal transactions between personality and occupational roles: A large and heterogeneous study of job beginners, stayers, and changers', *Developmental Psychology*, 50(7): 1931–42.

Denissen, J. J. A., Bleidorn, W., Hennecke, M., Luhmann, M., Orth, U., Specht, J. & Zimmermann, J. (2018) 'Uncovering the power of personality to shape income', *Psychological Science*, 29(1): 3–13.

DeYoung, C. G. (2006) 'Higher-order factors of the Big Five in a multi-informant sample', *Journal of Personality and Social Psychology*, 91(6): 1138–51.

DeYoung, C. G. (2010) 'Personality neuroscience and the biology of traits', *Social and Personality Psychology Compass*, 4(12): 1165–80.

Di Milia, L. (2004) 'Australian management selection practices: Closing the gap between research findings and practice', *Asia Pacific Journal of Human Resource*, 42(2): 214–28

Diener, E. & Lucas, R. E. (1999) 'Personality and subjective well-being', in D. Kahneman, E. Diener & N. Schwarz (eds), *Well-Being: Foundations of Hedonic Psychology* (pp 213–29), New York: Russell Sage Foundation.

Digman, J. M. (1990) 'Personality Structure: Emergence of the five-factor model', *Annual Review of Psychology*, 41(1): 417–40.

Digman, J. M. (1997) 'Higher-order factors of the Big Five', *Journal of Personality and Social Psychology*, 73(6): 1246–56.

Duan, J., Li, C., Xu, Y. & Wu, C. H. (2017) 'Transformational leadership and employee voice behavior: A Pygmalion mechanism', *Journal of Organizational Behavior*, 38(5): 650–70.

Dudley, N. M., Orvis, K. A., Lebiecki, J. E. & Cortina, J. M. (2006) 'A meta-analytic investigation of conscientiousness in the prediction of job performance: Examining the intercorrelations and the incremental validity of narrow traits', *Journal of Applied Psychology*, 91(1): 40–57.

Dunlop, W. L. (2015) 'Contextualized personality, beyond traits', *European Journal of Personality*, 29(3): 310–25.

Dweck, C. S. (2008) *Mindset: The New Psychology of Success*, New York: Random House.

Eccles, J. (2009) 'Who am I and what am I going to do with my life? Personal and collective identities as motivators of action', *Educational Psychologist*, 44(2): 78–89.

Eisenberger, R., Huntington, R., Hutchison, S. & Sowa, D. (1986) 'Perceived organizational support', *Journal of Applied Psychology*, 71(3): 500–7.

Eisenberger, R., Fasolo, P. & Davis-LaMastro, V. (1990) 'Perceived organizational support and employee diligence, commitment, and innovation', *Journal of Applied Psychology*, 75(1): 51–9.

Eisenberger, R., Armeli, S., Rexwinkel, B., Lynch, P. D. & Rhoades, L. (2001) 'Reciprocation of perceived organizational support', *Journal of Applied Psychology*, 86(1): 42–51.

Epitropaki, O. & Martin, R. (2005) 'From ideal to real: A longitudinal study of implicit leadership theories, leader–member exchanges and employee outcomes', *Journal of Applied Psychology*, 90(4): 659–76.

Erikson, E. H. (1950) *Child and Society*, New York: Norton.

Fiske, D. W. (1949) 'Consistency of the factorial structures of personality ratings from different sources', *Journal of Abnormal Psychology*, 44(3): 329–44.

Fleeson, W. (2001) 'Toward a structure- and process-integrated view of personality: Traits as density distributions of states', *Journal of Personality and Social Psychology*, 80(6): 1011–27.

Fleeson, W. (2004) 'Moving personality beyond the person-situation debate: The challenge and the opportunity of within-person variability', *Current Directions in Psychological Science*, 13: 83–7.

Fleeson, W. & Gallagher, P. (2009) 'The implications of Big Five standing for the distribution of trait manifestation in behavior: Fifteen experience-sampling studies and a meta-analysis', *Journal of Personality and Social Psychology*, 97(6): 1097–114.

Florida, R. (2002) *The Rise of the Creative Class*, New York: Basic Books.

Fraley, R. C. & Roberts, B. W. (2005) 'Patterns of continuity: A dynamic model for conceptualizing the stability of individual differences in psychological constructs across the life course', *Psychological Review*, 112(1): 60–74.

Franz, C. & White, K. W. (1985) 'Individuation and attachment in personality development: Extending Erikson's theory', *Journal of Personality*, 53(2): 224–57.

Fredrickson, B. L. (2001) 'The role of positive emotions in positive psychology', *American Psychologist*, 56(3): 218–26.

Frese, M. (1982) 'Occupational socialization and psychological development: An underemphasized research perspective in industrial psychology', *Journal of Occupational Psychology*, 55(3): 209–24.

Frese, M. & Zapf, D. (1994) 'Action as the core of work psychology: A German approach', in H. C. Triandis, M. D. Dunnette & L. M. Hough (eds), *Handbook of Industrial and Organizational Psychology* (2nd ed, Vol 4, pp 271–340), Palo Alto, CA: Consulting Psychologists Press.

Fuller, B. & Marler, L. E. (2009) 'Change driven by nature: A meta-analytic review of the proactive personality literature', *Journal of Vocational Behavior*, 75(3): 329–45.

Funder, D. C. (1991) 'Global traits: A neo-Allportian approach to personality', *Psychological Science*, 2(1): 31–9.

Funder, D. C. (1994) 'Explaining traits', *Psychological Inquiry*, 5(2): 125–127.

Funder, D. C. (1997) *The Personality Puzzle*, New York: Norton.

Furnham, A. (1992) *Personality at Work: The Role of Individual Differences in the Workplace*, London: Routledge.

Furnham, A. (2016) 'Eysenck at work: The application of his theories to work psychology', *Personality and Individual Differences*, 103: 148–52.

Galton, F. (1884) 'Measurement of character', *Fortnightly Review*, 36: 179–85.

Gecas, V. & Seff, M. A. (1989) 'Social class, occupational conditions, and self-esteem', *Sociological Perspectives*, 32(3): 353–64.

Geukes, K., van Zalk, M. & Back, M. D. (2017) 'Analysing processes in personality development', in J. Specht (ed), *Personality Development across the Lifespan* (pp 455–472), San Diego: Elsevier.

Geukes, K., van Zalk, M. & Back, M. D. (2018) 'Understanding personality development: An integrative state process model', *International Journal of Behavioral Development*, 42(1): 43–51.

Gioia, D. A., Patvardhan, S. D., Hamilton, A. L. & Corley, K. G. (2013) 'Organizational identity formation and change', *Academy of Management Annals*, 7(1): 123–93.

Goldberg, L. R. (1990) 'An alternative "description of personality": The Big-Five factor structure', *Journal of Personality and Social Psychology*, 59(6): 1216–29.

Goldberg, L. R. (1993) 'The structure of phenotypic personality traits: Authors' reactions to the six comments', *American Psychologist*, 48(12): 1303–04.

Gong, Y., Huang, J. C. & Farh, J. L. (2009) 'Employee learning orientation, transformational leadership, and employee creativity: The mediating role of employee creative self-efficacy', *The Academy of Management Journal*, 52: 765–78.

Graen, G. B. & Uhl-Bien, M. (1995) 'Relationship-based approach to leadership: Development of leader–member exchange (LMX) theory of leadership over 25 years: Applying a multi-level multi-domain perspective', *The Leadership Quarterly*, 6(2): 219–47.

Grant, A. M. (2007) 'Job design and the motivation to make a prosocial difference', *The Academy of Management Review*, 32(2): 393–417.

Grant, A. M. & Parker, S. K. (2009) '7 Redesigning work design theories: The rise of relational and proactive perspectives', *The Academy of Management Annals*, 3(1): 317–75.

Grijalva, E. & Newman, D. A. (2015) 'Narcissism and counterproductive work behavior (CWB): Meta-analysis and consideration of collectivist culture, Big Five personality, and Narcissism's facet structure', *Applied Psychology*, 64(1): 93–126.

Guion, R. M. & Gottier, R. F. (1965) 'Validity of personality measures in personnel selection', *Personnel Psychology*, 18(2): 135–64.

Hackman, J. R. & Oldham, G. R. (1975) 'Development of the job diagnostic survey', *Journal of Applied Psychology*, 60(2): 159–70.

Hackman, J. R. & Oldham, G. R. (1976) 'Motivation through the design of work: Test of a theory', *Organizational Behavior and Human Performance*, 16: 250–279.

Hall, D. T. & Las Heras, M. (2010) 'Reintegrating job design and career theory: Creating not just good jobs but smart jobs', *Journal of Organizational Behavior*, 31(2): 448–62.

Hammond, M. M., Neff, N. L., Farr, J. L., Schwall, A. R. & Zhao, X. (2011) 'Predictors of individual-level innovation at work: A meta-analysis', *Psychology of Aesthetics, Creativity, and the Arts*, 5(1): 90–105.

Hampson, S. E. & Goldberg, L. R. (2006) 'A first large cohort study of personality trait stability over the 40 years between elementary school and midlife', *Journal of Personality and Social Psychology*, 91(4): 763–79.

Harms, P. D., Roberts, B. W. & Winter, D. (2006) 'Becoming the Harvard man: Person–environment fit, personality development, and academic success', *Personality and Social Psychology Bulletin*, 32(7): 851–65.

Harrell, E. (2017) 'A brief history of personality tests', *Harvard Business Review*, March–April, Available from: https://hbr.org/2017/03/the-new-science-of-team-chemistry

Harris, M. A., Brett, C. E., Johnson, W. & Deary, I. J. (2016) 'Personality stability from age 14 to age 77 years', *Psychology and Aging*, 31(8): 862–74.

Heatherton, T. F. & Nichols, P. A. (1994) 'Conceptual issues in assessing whether personality can change', in T. F. Heatherton & J. L. Weinberger (eds), *Can Personality Change?* (pp 3–18), Washington, DC: American Psychological Association.

Helson, R. & Wink, P. (1992) 'Personality change in women from the early 40s to the early 50s', *Psychology and Aging*, 7(1): 46–55.

Helson, R., Roberts, B. & Agronick, G. (1995) 'Enduringness and change in creative personality and the prediction of occupational creativity', *Journal of Personality and Social Psychology*, 69(6): 1173–83.

Hennecke, M., Bleidorn, W., Denissen, J. J. A. & Wood, D. (2014) 'A three-part framework for self-regulated personality development across adulthood', *European Journal of Personality*, 28: 289–99.

Hoekstra, H. A. (2011) 'A career roles model of career development', *Journal of Vocational Behavior*, 78(2): 159–73.

Hogan, J. & Holland, B. (2003) 'Using theory to evaluate personality and job-performance relations: A socioanalytic perspective', *Journal of Applied Psychology*, 88(1): 100–12.

Hogan, J. & Roberts, B. W. (1996) 'Issues and non-issues in the fidelity-bandwidth trade-off', *Journal of Organizational Behavior*, 17(6): 627–37.

Hogan, R. (2007) *Personality and the Fate of Organizations* Mahwah, NJ: Lawrence Erlbaum Associates.

Hogan, R. & Roberts, B. W. (2004) 'A socioanalytic model of personality', *Journal of Career Assessment*, 12(2): 207–17.

Holland, J. L. (1959) 'A theory of vocational choice', *Journal of Counseling Psychology*, 6(1): 35–45.

Holland, J. L. (1997) *Making Vocational Choices: A Theory of Vocational Personalities and Work Environments* (3rd edn), Odessa: Psychological Assessment Resources.

Hough, L. M. (1992) 'The 'Big Five' personality variables – construct confusion: Description versus prediction', *Human Performance*, 5(1/2): 139–55.

House, J. S. (1981) 'Social structure and personality', in M. Rosenberg & R. H. Turner (eds), *Social Psychology: Sociological Perspectives* (pp 525–61), New York: Basic Books.

Howard, A. & Bray, D. W. (1988) *Managerial Lives in Transition: Advancing Age and Changing Times*, New York: Guilford Press.

Hudson, N. W. & Fraley, R. C. (2015) 'Volitional personality trait change: Can people choose to change their personality traits?', *Journal of Personality and Social Psychology*, 109(3): 490–507.

Hudson, N. W. & Fraley, R. C. (2016a) 'Changing for the better? Longitudinal associations between volitional personality change and psychological well-being', *Personality and Social Psychology Bulletin*, 42(5): 603–15.

Hudson, N. W. & Fraley, R. C. (2016b) 'Do people's desires to change their personality traits vary with age? An examination of trait change goals across adulthood', *Social Psychological and Personality Science*, 7(8): 847–56.

Hudson, N. W. & Fraley, R. C. (2017) 'Volitional personality change', in J. Specht (ed), *Personality Development across the Lifespan* (pp 555–71), San Diego: Elsevier.

Hudson, N. W. & Roberts, B. W. (2014) 'Goals to change personality traits: Concurrent links between personality traits, daily behavior, and goals to change oneself', *Journal of Research in Personality*, 53: 68–83.

Hudson, N. W. & Roberts, B. W. (2016) 'Social investment in work reliably predicts change in conscientiousness and agreeableness: A direct replication and extension of Hudson, Roberts, and Lodi-Smith (2012)', *Journal of Research in Personality*, 60: 12–23.

Hudson, N. W., Roberts, B. W. & Lodi-Smith, J. (2012) 'Personality trait development and social investment in work', *Journal of Research in Personality*, 46(3): 334–44.

Hudson, N. W., Briley, D. A., Chopik, W. J. & Derringer, J. (2019) 'You have to follow through: Attaining behavioural change goals predicts volitional personality change', *Journal of Personality and Social Psychology*, 117(4): 839–57.

Hudson, N. W., Fraley, R. C., Chopik, W. J. & Briley, D. A. (2020) 'Change goals robustly predict trait growth: A mega-analysis of a dozen intensive longitudinal studies examining volitional change', *Social Psychological and Personality Science*, 11(6): 723–32.

Humphrey, S. E., Nahrgang, J. D. & Morgeson, F. P. (2007) 'Integrating motivational, social, and contextual work design features: A meta-analytic summary and theoretical extension of the work design literature', *Journal of Applied Psychology*, 92(5): 1332–56.

Hurtz, G. M. & Donovan, J. J. (2000) 'Personality and job performance: The Big Five revisited', *Journal of Applied Psychology*, 85(6): 869–79.

Hutteman, R., Bleidorn, W., Kereteš, G., Brković, I., Butković, A. & Denissen, J. J. A. (2014) 'Reciprocal associations between parenting challenges and parents' personality development in young and middle adulthood', *European Journal of Personality*, 28(2): 168–79.

Ibarra, H. (1999) 'Provisional selves: Experimenting with image and identity in professional adaptation', *Administrative Science Quarterly*, 44(4): 764–91.

Jackson, J. J., Hill, P. L., Payne, B. R., Roberts, B. W. & Stine-Morrow, E. A. L. (2012a) 'Can an old dog learn (and want to experience) new tricks? Cognitive training increases openness to experience in older adults', *Psychology and Aging*, 27(2): 286–92.

Jackson, J. J., Thoemmes, F., Jonkmann, K., Lüdtke, O. & Trautwein, U. (2012b) 'Military training and personality trait development: Does the military make the man, or does the man make the military?', *Psychological Science*, 23(3): 270–7.

James, W. (1890) *Principles of Psychology*, New York: Holt.

Jayawickreme, E. & Blackie, L. E. (2014) 'Post-Traumatic Growth as Positive Personality Change: Evidence, Controversies and Future Directions', *European Journal of Personality*, 28(4): 312–32.

Jokela, M. (2017) 'Personality and social structure', *European Journal of Personality*, 31(3): 205–7.

Josefsson, K., Jokela, M., Cloninger, C. R., Hintsanen, M., Salo, J., Hintsa, T. & Keltikangas-Jarvinen, L. (2013) 'Maturity and change in personality: developmental trends of temperament and character in adulthood', *Development and Psychopathology*, 25(3): 713–27.

Judge, T. A. & Bono, J. E. (2001) 'Relationship of core self-evaluations traits—self-esteem, generalized self-efficacy, locus of control, and emotional stability—with job satisfaction and job performance: A meta-analysis', *Journal of Applied Psychology*, 86(1): 80–92.

Judge, T. A. & Kammeyer-Mueller, J. D. (2011) 'Implications of core self-evaluations for a changing organizational context', *Human Resource Management Review*, 21(4): 331–41.

Judge, T. A., Bono, J. E., Remus, I. & Gerhardt, M. W. (2002a) 'Personality and leadership: A qualitative and quantitative review', *Journal of Applied Psychology*, 87(4): 765–80.

Judge, T. A., Erez, A., Bono, J. E. & Thoresen, C. J. (2002b) 'Are measures of self-esteem, neuroticism, locus of control, and generalized self-efficacy indicators of a common core construct?', *Journal of Personality and Social Psychology*, 83(3): 693–710.

Judge, T. A., Heller, D. & Mount, M. K. (2002c) 'Five-factor model of personality and job satisfaction: A meta-analysis', *Journal of Applied Psychology*, 87(3): 530–41.

Kandler, C., Zimmermann, J. & McAdams, D. P. (2014) 'Core and surface characteristics for the description and theory of personality differences and development', *European Journal of Personality*, 28(3): 231–43.

Karasek, R. A. (1979) 'Job demands, job decision latitude and mental strain: Implications for job redesign', *Administrative Science Quarterly*, 24: 285–306.

Karasek, R. A., Brisson, C., Kawakami, N., Houtman, I., Bongers, P. & Amick, B. (1998) 'The Job Content Questionnaire (JCQ): An instrument for internationally comparative assessments of psycho-social job characteristics', *Journal of Occupational Health Psychology*, 3(4): 322–55.

Kinley, N. & Ben-Hur, S. (2013) *Talent Intelligence: What You Need to Know to Identify and Measure Talent*, San Francisco: Jossey-Bass.

Kohn, M. L. (1976) 'Occupational structure and alienation', *American Journal of Sociology*, 82(1): 111–30.

Kohn, M. L. (1989) 'Social structure and personality: A quintessentially sociological approach to social psychology', *Social Forces*, 68(1): 26–33.

Kohn, M. L. & Schooler, C. (1973) 'Occupational experience and psychological functioning: An assessment of reciprocal effects', *American Sociological Review*, 38(1): 97–118.

Kohn, M. L. & Schooler, C. (1978) 'The reciprocal effects of the substantive complexity of work and intellectual flexibility: A longitudinal assessment', *American Journal of Sociology*, 84: 24–52.

Kohn, M. L. & Schooler, C. (1982) 'Job conditions and personality: A longitudinal assessment of their reciprocal effects', *American Journal of Sociology*, 87: 1257–86.

Kohn, M. L., Zaborowski, W., Janicka, K., Mach, B. W., Khmelko, V., Slomczynski, K. M. & Podobnik, B. (2000) 'Complexity of activities and personality under conditions of radical social change: A comparative analysis of Poland and Ukraine', *Social Psychology Quarterly*, 63(3): 187–207.

Krasner, M. S., Epstein, R. M., Beckman, H., Suchman, A. L., Chapman, B., Mooney, C. J. & Quill, T. E. (2009) 'Association of an educational program in mindful communication with burnout, empathy, and attitudes among primary care physicians', *Journal of the American Medical Association*, 302(12): 1284–93.

Kroeck, K. G. & Brown, K. W. (2003) 'Work applications of the Big Five model of personality', in M. Hersen (ed.), *Comprehensive Handbook of Psychological Assessment* (Vol 4, pp 109–29). Hoboken, NJ: John Wiley & Sons.

Kruglanski, A. W. (1996) 'Goals as knowledge structures', In P. M. Gollwitzer & J. A. Bargh (eds), *The Psychology of Action: Linking Cognition and Motivation to Behavior* (p 599–618), New York: Guilford Press.

LaRosa, J. (2018) 'What's next for the $9.9 billion personal development industry', *Market Research*, Blog, 27 January, Available from: https://blog.marketresearch.com/whats-next-for-the-9-9-billion-personal-development-industry

Le, K., Donnellan, M. B. & Conger, R. (2014) 'Personality development at work: Workplace conditions, personality changes, and the corresponsive principle', *Journal of Personality*, 82(1): 44–56.

Lee, K. & Ashton, M. C. (2008) 'The HEXACO personality factors in the indigenous personality lexicons of English and 11 other languages', *Journal of Personality*, 76(5): 1001–53.

Lee, K. & Ashton, M. C. (2012) *The H Factor of Personality*, Waterloo, Canada: Wilfrid Laurier University Press.

Lee, Y., Berry, C. M. & Gonzalez-Mulé, E. (2019) 'The importance of being humble: A meta-analysis and incremental validity analysis of the relationship between honesty-humility and job performance', *Journal of Applied Psychology*, 104(12): 1535–46.

Lehnart, J., Neyer, F. J. & Eccles, J. (2010) 'Long-Term Effects of Social Investment: The Case of Partnering in Young Adulthood', *Journal of Personality*, 78(2): 639–70.

LePine, J. A., Erez, A. & Johnson, D. E. (2002) 'The nature and dimensionality of organizational citizenship behavior: A critical review and meta-analysis', *Journal of Applied Psychology*, 87(1): 52–65.

LePine, J. A., Buckman, B. R., Crawford, E. R. & Methot, J. R. (2011) 'A review of research on personality in teams: Accounting for pathways spanning levels of theory and analysis', *Human Resource Management Review*, 21(4): 311–330.

Levinson, D. J., Darrow, D. N., Klein, E. B., Levinson, M. H. & McKee, B. (1978) *The Seasons of a Man's Life*, New York: Knopf.

Li, W. D., Fay, D., Frese, M., Harms, P. D. & Gao, X. Y. (2014) 'Reciprocal relationship between proactive personality and work characteristics: A latent change score approach', *Journal of Applied Psychology*, 99(5): 948–65.

Li, W. D., Li, S., Fay, D. & Frese, M. (2019) 'Reciprocal relationships between dispositional optimism and work experiences: A five wave longitudinal investigation', *Journal of Applied Psychology*, 104(12): 1471–86.

Li, W. D., Li, S., Feng, J., Wang, M., Zhang, H., Frese, M. & Wu, C. H. (2020) 'Can becoming a leader change your personality? An investigation with two longitudinal studies from a role-based perspective', *Journal of Applied Psychology*, Available from: https://doi.org/10.1037/apl0000808

Lincoln, J. R. & McBride, K. (1987) 'Japanese industrial organization in comparative perspective', *Annual Review of Sociology*, 13(1): 289–312.

Locke, E. A. (1969) 'What is job satisfaction?', *Organization Behavior and Human Performance*, 4(4): 309–36.

Locke, E. A. (1976) 'The nature and causes of job satisfaction', in M. D. Dunnette (ed), *Handbook of Industrial and Organizational Psychology* (pp 1297–343), Chicago: Rand McNally.

Locke, E. A. & Hulin, C. L. (1962) 'A review and evaluation of the validity studies of Activity Vector Analysis', *Personnel Psychology*, 15(2): 25–42.

Löckenhoff, C. E., Terracciano, A. & Costa, P. T. (2009) 'Five-factor model personality traits and the retirement transition: Longitudinal and cross-sectional association', *Psychology and Aging*, 24(3): 722–8.

Lodi-Smith, J. & Roberts, B. W. (2007) 'Social investment and personality: A meta-analysis of the relationship of personality traits to investment in work, family, religion, and volunteerism', *Personality and Social Psychology Review*, 11(1): 68–86.

Lord, R. G., Brown, D. J. & Freiberg, S. J. (1999) 'Understanding the dynamics of leadership: The role of follower self-concepts in the leader/follower relationship', *Organizational Behavior and Human Decision Processes*,78(3): 167–203.

Lucas, R. E. & Donnellan, M. B. (2011) 'Personality development across the life span: Longitudinal analyses with a national sample from Germany', *Journal of Personality and Social Psychology*, 101(4): 847–61.

Lüdtke, O., Roberts, B. W., Trautwein, U. & Nagy, G. (2011) 'A random walk down university avenue: Life paths, life events, and personality trait change at the transition to university', *Journal of Personality and Social Psychology*, 101(3): 620–37.

Luhmann, M., Orth, U., Specht, J., Kandler, C. & Lucas, R. E. (2014) 'Studying changes in life circumstances and changes in personality: It's about time', *European Journal of Personality*, 28(3): 256–66.

Luthans, F., Youssef, C. M. & Avolio, B. J. (2007) *Psychological capital*, New York: Oxford University Press.

Lynch, M. F., Vansteenkiste, M., Deci, E. L. & Ryan, R. M. (2011) 'Autonomy as process and outcome: Revisiting cultural and practical issues in motivation for counseling', *The Counseling Psychologist*, 39(2): 286–302.

Ma, H. H. (2009) 'The effect size of variables associated with creativity: A meta-analysis', *Creativity Research Journal*, 21(1): 30–42.

Magidson, J. F., roberts, B. W., Collado-rodriguez, A. & Lejuez, C. W. (2014) 'Theory-driven intervention for changing personality: expectancy value theory, behavioral activation, and conscientiousness', *Developmental Psychology*, 50(5): 1442–50.

Markus, H. & Nurius, P. (1986) 'Possible selves', *American Psychologist*, 41: 954–69.

Martin, L. S., Oades, L. G. & Caputi, P. (2014a) 'Intentional personality change coaching: A randomised controlled trial of participant selected personality facet change using the Five-Factor Model of Personality', *International Coaching Psychology Review*, 9(2): 196–209.

Martin, L. S., Oades, L. G. & Caputi, P. (2014b) 'A step-wise process of intentional personality change coaching', *International Coaching Psychology Review*, 9(2): 167–81.

McAdams, D. P. & Olson, B. D. (2010) 'Personality development: Continuity and change over the life course', *Annual Review of Psychology*, 61(1): 517–42.

McCrae, R. R. & Costa, P. T. (1997) 'Personality trait structures as a human universal', *American Psychologist*, 52(5): 509–16.

McCrae, R. R. & Costa, P. T. (2003) *Personality in Adulthood: A Five-Factor Theory Perspective* (2nd edn), New York: Guilford Press.

McCrae, R. R. & Costa, P. T. (2008) 'The five-factor theory of personality', in O. P. John, R. W. Robins & L. A. Pervin (eds), *Handbook of Personality: Theory and Research* (pp 159–81), New York: Guilford Press.

McCrae, R. R. & Terracciano, A. (2005) 'Universal features of personality traits from the observer's perspective: Data from 50 cultures', *Journal of Personality and Social Psychology*, 88(3): 547–61.

McLeod, J. D. & Lively, K. J. (2006) 'Social structure and personality', in J. Delamater (ed), *Handbook of Social Psychology* (pp 77–102), Boston, MA: Springer.

Miller, T. J., Baranski, E. N., Dunlop, W. L. & Ozer, D. J. (2019) 'Striving for change: The prevalence and correlates of personality change goals', *Journal of Research in Personality*, 80: 10–6.

Mischel, W. (1968) *Personality and Assessment*, New York: Wiley.

Morey, L. C. & Hopwood, C. J. (2013) 'Stability and Change in Personality Disorders', *Annual Review of Clinical Psychology*, 9(1): 499–528.

Morgeson, F. P. & Humphrey, S. E. (2006) 'The work design questionnaire (WDQ): Developing and validating a comprehensive measure for assessing job design and the nature of work', *Journal of Applied Psychology*, 91(6): 1321–39.

Mortimer, J. T. & Lorence, J. (1979) 'Occupational experience and the self-concept: A longitudinal study', *Social Psychology Quarterly*, 42(4): 307–23.

Mount, M. K. & Barrick, M. R. (1995) 'The big five personality dimensions: Implications for research and practice in human resources management', in Gerald R. Ferris (ed), *Research in Personnel and Human Resources Management* (Vol 13, pp 153–201), Oxford: JAI Press/Elsevier Science.

Mount, M. K., Barrick, M. R. & Stewart, G. L. (1998) 'Five-Factor Model of personality and Performance in Jobs Involving Interpersonal Interaction',. *Human Performance*, 11(2): 145–65.

Mroczek, D. K. (2014) 'Personality plasticity, healthy aging, and interventions', *Developmental Psychology*, 50(5): 1470–4.

Mroczek, D. K. & Spiro, A. (2003) 'Modeling intraindividual change in personality traits: Findings from the normative aging study', *The Journals of Gerontology: Series B*, 58(3): 153–65.

Mroczek, D. K. & Spiro, A. (2007) 'Personality Change Influences Mortality in Older Men', *Psychological Science,* 18(5): 371–6.

Mroczek, D. K., Almeida, D. M., Spiro, A. & Pafford, C. (2006) 'Modeling intraindividual stability and change in personality', in D. K. Mroczek & T. D. Little (eds), *Handbook of Personality Development* (pp 163–80), Mahwah, NJ: Lawrence Erlbaum Associates.

Nelis, D., Kotsou, I., Quoidbach, J., Hansenne, M., Weytens, F., Dupuis, P. & Mikolajczak, M. (2011) 'Increasing emotional competence improves psychological and physical well-being, social relationships, and employability', *Emotion*, 11(2): 354–66.

Neugarten, B. L. & Datan, N. (1973/1996) 'Sociological perspectives on the life cycle', in D. A. Neugarten (ed), *The Meanings of Age: Selected Papers of Bernice L. Neugarten* (pp 96–113), Chicago: University of Chicago Press.

Neugarten, B. L., Moore, J. W. & Lowe, J. C. (1965) 'Age norms, age constraints, and adult socialization', *American Journal of Sociology*, 70(6): 710–7.

Newton, N. & Stewart, A. J. (2010) 'The Middle Ages: Change in Women's Personalities and Social Roles', *Psychology of Women Quarterly*, 34(1): 75–84.

Neyer, F. J. & Asendorpf, J. B. (2001) 'Personality–relationship transaction in young adulthood', *Journal of Personality and Social Psychology*, 81(6): 1190–204.

Neyer, F. J. & Lehnart, J. (2007) 'Relationships matter in personality development: Evidence from an 8-year longitudinal study across young adulthood', *Journal of Personality*, 75(3): 535–68.

Ng, T. W. H., Sorensen, K. L. & Eby, L. T. (2006) 'Locus of control at work: a meta-analysis. *Journal of Organizational Behavior*, 27(8): 1057–87.

Nieß, C. & Zacher, H. (2015) 'Openness to experience as a predictor and outcome of upward job changes into managerial and professional positions', *PLOS One*, 10(6), e0131115.

Norman, W. T. (1963) 'Toward an adequate taxonomy of personality attributes: Replicated factor structure in peer nomination personality ratings', *The Journal of Abnormal and Social Psychology*, 66(6): 574–83.

O'Boyle, E. H., Jr., Forsyth, D. R., Banks, G. C. & McDaniel, M. A. (2012) 'A meta-analysis of the Dark Triad and work behavior: A social exchange perspective', *Journal of Applied Psychology*, 97(3): 557–79.

Ones, D. S. & Viswesvaran, C. (1996) 'Bandwidth–fidelity dilemma in personality measurement for personnel selection', *Journal of Organizational Behavior*, 17(6): 609–26.

Ones, D. S., Viswesvaran, C. & Dilchert, S. (2005) 'Personality at Work: Raising Awareness and Correcting Misconceptions', *Human Performance*, 18(4): 389–404.

Organ, D. W. & Ryan, K. (1995) 'A meta-analytical review of attitudinal and dispositional predictors of organizational citizenship behavior', *Personnel Psychology*, 48(4): 775–802.

Orth, U., Robins, R. W. & Widaman, K. F. (2012) 'Life-span development of self-esteem and its effects on important life outcomes', *Journal of Personality and Social Psychology*, 102(6): 1271–88.

Orvis, K. A., Dudley, N. M. & Cortina, J. M. (2008) 'Conscientiousness and reactions to psychological contract breach: A longitudinal field study', *Journal of Applied Psychology*, 93(5): 1183–93.

Parker, S. K. & Turner, N. (2002) 'Work design and individual job performance: Research findings and an agenda for future inquiry', in S. Sonnentag (ed), *Psychological Management of Individual Performance*, Chichester: John Wiley & Sons.

Paul, A. M. (2004) *The Cult of Personality: How Personality Tests Are Leading Us to Miseducate Our Children, Mismanage Our Companies, and Misunderstand Ourselves*, New York: Free Press.

Pervin, L. A. (1994) 'Personality stability, personality change, and the question of process'. In T. F. Heatherton & J. L. Weinberger (Eds.), Can personality change? (pp. 315–30). Washington, DC: American Psychological Association.

Pletzer, J. L., Bentvelzen, M., Oostom, J. K. & de Vries, R. E. (2019) 'A meta-analysis of the relations between personality and workplace deviance: Big Five versus HEXACO', *Journal of Vocational Behavior*, 122: 369–83.

Quintus, M., Egloff, B. & Wrzus, C. (2017) 'Predictors of volitional personality change in younger and older adults: Response surface analyses signify the complementary perspectives of the self and knowledgeable others', *Journal of Research in Personality*, 70: 214–28.

Quintus, M., Egloff, B. & Wrzus, C. (2020) 'Daily life processes predict long-term development in explicit and implicit representations of Big Five traits: Testing predictions from the TESSERA (Triggering Situations, Expectancies, States and State Expressions, and ReActions) framework', *Journal of Personality and Social Psychology*, Available from: http://dx.doi.org/10.1037/pspp0000361

Richter, J., Brändström, S., Emami, H. & Ghazinour, S. (2004) 'Temperament and character in cross-cultural comparisons between Swedish and Iranian people and Iranian refugees in Sweden–personality in transition?', *Collegium Antropologicum Biological Anthropology*, 28(2): 865–76.

Roberts, B. W. (1997) 'Plaster or plasticity: Are adult work experiences associated with personality change in women?', *Journal of Personality*, 65(2): 205–32.

Roberts, B. W. (2006) 'Personality development and organizational behavior', in B. M. Staw (ed), *Research on Organizational Behavior* (pp 1–41), Oxford: Elsevier Science/JAI Press.

Roberts, B. W. (2009) 'Back to the future: Personality and Assessment and personality development', *Journal of Research in Personality*, 43(2): 137–45.

Roberts, B. W. (2018) 'A revised sociogenomic model of personality traits', *Journal of Personality*, 86(1): 23–35.

Roberts, B. W. & DelVecchio, W. F. (2000) 'The rank-order consistency of personality traits from childhood to old age: A quantitative review of longitudinal studies', *Psychological Bulletin*, 126(1): 3–25.

Roberts, B. W. & Jackson, J. J. (2008) 'Sociogenomic personality psychology', *Journal of Personality*, 76(6): 1523–44.

Roberts, B. W. & Mroczek, D. (2008) 'Personality trait change in adulthood', *Current Directions in Psychological Science*, 17(1): 31–5.

Roberts, B. W. & Nickel, L. W. (2017) 'A critical evaluation of the neo-socioanalytic model of personality', in J. Specht (ed), *Personality Development across the Lifespan* (pp 157–77), San Diego: Elsevier.

Roberts, B. W. & Wood, D. (2006) 'Personality development in the context of the neo-socioanalytic model of personality', in D. Mroczek & T. D. Little (eds), *Handbook of Personality Development* (pp 11–39), Mahwah, NJ, US: Lawrence Erlbaum Associates Publishers.

Roberts, B. W., Caspi, A. & Moffitt, T. E. (2003) 'Work experiences and personality development in young adulthood', *Journal of Personality and Social Psychology*, 84(3): 582–93.

Roberts, B. W., O'Donnell, M. & Robins, R. W. (2004) 'Goal and Personality Trait Development in Emerging Adulthood', *Journal of Personality and Social Psychology*, 87(4): 541–50.

Roberts, B. W., Wood, D. & Lodi-Smith, J. L. (2005) 'Evaluating Five Factor Theory and social investment perspectives on personality trait development', *Journal of Research in Personality*, 39(1): 166–84.

Roberts, B. W., Walton, K. & Viechtbauer, W. (2006) 'Patterns of mean-level change in personality traits across the life course: A meta-analysis of longitudinal studies', *Psychological Bulletin*, 132(1): 1–25.

Roberts, B. W., Kuncel, N. R., Shiner, R., Caspi, A. & Goldberg, L. R. (2007) 'The power of personality: The comparative validity of personality traits, socioeconomic status, and cognitive ability for predicting important life outcomes', *Perspectives on Psychological Science*, 2(4): 313–45.

Roberts, B. W., Wood, D. & Caspi, A. (2008) 'The development of personality traits in adulthood', in O. P. John (ed), *Handbook of Personality: Theory and Research* (3rd edn, pp 375–98). New York: Guilford Press.

Roberts, B. W., Donnellan, M. B. & Hill, P. L. (2012) 'Personality trait development in adulthood: Findings and implications', in I. B. Weiner, H. Tennen & J. M. Suls (eds), *Handbook of Psychology; Volume 5: Personality and Social Psychology*, New York: Wiley.

Roberts, B. W., Luo, J., Briley, D. A., Chow, P. I., Su, R. & Hill, P. L. (2017) 'A systematic review of personality trait change through intervention', *Psychological Bulletin*, 143(2): 117–41.

Robins, R. W., Noftle, E. E., Trzesniewski, K. H. & Roberts, B. W. (2005) 'Do people know how their personality has changed? Correlates of perceived and actual personality change in young adulthood', *Journal of Personality*, 73(2): 489–521.

Robinson, O. C., Noftle, E. E., Guo, J., Asadi, S. & Zhang, X. (2015) 'Goals and plans for Big Five personality trait change in young adults', *Journal of Research in Personality*, 59: 31–43.

Rollnick, S., Mason, P. & Butler, C. (1999) *Health Behaviour Change: A Guide for Practitioners*, Edinburgh: Churchill Livingstone.

Rousseau, D. M. (1990) 'New hire perceptions of their own and their employer's obligations: A study of psychological contracts', *Journal of Organizational Behavior*, 11(5): 389–400.

Ryan, R. M. & Deci, E. L. (2008) 'A self-determination theory approach to psychotherapy: The motivational basis for effective change', *Canadian Psychology*, 49(3): 186–93.

Ryff, C. D. (1987) 'The place of personality and social structure research in social psychology', *Journal of Personality and Social Psychology*, 53(6): 1192–202.

Salgado, J. F. (1997) 'The five-factor model of personality and job performance in the European community', *Journal of Applied Psychology*, 76(4): 613–27.

Salgado, J. F. (2002) 'The Big Five personality dimensions and counterproductive behaviors', *International Journal of Selection and Assessment*, 10(1–2): 117–125.

Salgado, J. F. & De Fruyt, F. (2005) 'Personality in personnel selection', in A. Evers, N. Anderson & O. Voskuijl (eds), *The Blackwell Handbook of Personnel Selection* (pp 174–98), London: Blackwell.

Scarr, S. & McCartney, K. (1983) 'How people make their own environments: A theory of genotype→environment effects', *Child Development*, 54(2): 424–35.

Schaufeli, W. B. & Bakker, A. B. (2004) 'Job demands, job resources, and their relationship with burnout and engagement: A multi-sample study', *Journal of Organizational Behavior*, 25(3): 293–315.

Schmidt, F. L. & Hunter, J. E. (1998) 'The validity and utility of selection methods in personnel research: Practical and theoretical implications of 85 years of research findings', *Psychological Bulletin*, 124(2): 262–74.

Schmitt, N., Gooding, R. Z., Noe, R. A. & Kirsch, M. (1984) 'Meta-analysis of validity studies published between 1964 and 1982 and the investigation of study characteristics', *Personnel Psychology*, 37(3): 407–22.

Schneider, B. (1987) 'The people make the place', *Personnel Psychology*, 40(3): 437–53.

Schunk, D. H. & Usher, E. L. (2012) 'Social cognitive theory and motivation' in R. M. Ryan (ed), *The Oxford Handbook of Human Motivation* (pp 13–27), New York, NY: Oxford University Press.

Scollon, C. N. & Diener, E. (2006) 'Love, work, and changes in extraversion and neuroticism over time', *Journal of Personality and Social Psychology*, 91(6): 1152–65.

Sedlmeier, P., Eberth, J., Schwarz, M., Zimmermann, D., Haarig, F., Jaeger, S. & Kunze, S. (2012) 'The psychological effects of meditation: A meta-analysis', *Psychological Bulletin*, 138(6): 1139–71.

Shamir, B. (1991) 'Meaning, self and motivation in organizations', *Organization Studies*, 12(3): 405–24.

Shamir, B., House, R. J. & Arthur, M. B. (1993) 'The motivational effects of charismatic leadership: A self-concept based theory', *Organization Science*, 4(4): 577–94.

Shore, L. M. & Coyle-Shapiro, J. A. M. (2003) 'New developments in the employee–organization relationship', *Journal of Organizational Behavior*, 24(5): 443–50.

Shore, L. M., Coyle-Shapiro, J. A. M. & Tetrick, L. E. (2012) *The Employee-Organization Relationship: Applications for the 21st Century*, London: Routledge Academic.

Specht, J., Egloff, B. & Schmukle, S. C. (2011) 'Stability and change of personality across the life course: The impact of age and major life events on mean-level and rank-order stability of the Big Five', *Journal of Personality and Social Psychology*, 101(4): 862–82.

Specht, J., Bleidorn, W., Denissen, J. J. A., Hennecke, M., Hutteman, R., Kandler, C. et al (2014a). What Drives Adult Personality Development? A Comparison of Theoretical Perspectives and Empirical Evidence', *European Journal of Personality*, 28(3): 216–30.

Specht, J., Luhmann, M. & Geiser, C. (2014b) 'On the consistency of personality types across adulthood: Latent profile analyses in two large-scale panel studies', *Journal of Personality and Social Psychology*, 107(3): 540–56.

Spence, G. B. & Grant, A. M. (2005) 'Individual and group life-coaching: initial findings from a randomised, controlled trial', in M. Cavanagh, A. M. Grant & T. Kemp (eds), *Evidence-Based Coaching* (Vol 1, pp143–58), Bowen Hills, Australia: Australian Academic Press.

Spenner, K. I. (1988) 'Social stratification, work, and personality', *Annual Review of Sociology*, 14(1): 69–97.

Stajkovic, A. D. & Luthans, F. (1998) 'Self-efficacy and work-related performance: A meta-analysis', *Psychological Bulletin*, 124(2): 240–61.

Staudinger, U. M. & Kunzmann, U. (2005) 'Positive adult personality development: Adjustment and/or growth?', *European Psychology*, 10(4): 320–9.

Steel, P., Schmidt, J. & Shultz, J. (2008) 'Refining the relationship between personality and subjective well-being', *Psychological Bulletin*, 134(1): 138–61.

Stewart, A. J. & Vandewater, E. A. (1993) 'The Radcliffe class of 1964: Career and family social clock projects in a transitional cohort', in K. D. Hulbert & D. T. Schuster (eds), *Women's Lives Through Time: Educated American Women of the Twentieth Century* (p 235–58), San Fransico, US: Jossey-Bass.

Stieger, M., Wepfer, S., Rüegger, D., Kowatsch, T., Roberts, B. W. & Allemand, M. (2020) 'Becoming more conscientious or more open to experience? Effects of a two-week smartphone-based intervention for personality change', *European Journal of Personality*, 34(3): 345–66.

Stoll, G. & Trautwein, U. (2017) 'Vocational interests as personality traits: Characteristics, development, and significance in educational and organizational environments', in J. Specht (ed), *Personality Development across the Lifespan* (pp 401–17), San Diego: Elsevier.

Strauss, K., Griffin, M. A. & Parker, S. K. (2012) 'Future work selves: How salient hoped-for identities motivate proactive career behaviors', *Journal of Applied Psychology*, 97(3): 580–98.

Sutin, A. R. & Costa, P. T. (2010) 'Reciprocal influences of personality and job characteristics across middle adulthood', *Journal of Personality*, 78(1): 257–88.

Sutin, A. R., Costa, P. T., Miech, R. & Eaton, W. W. (2009) 'Personality and career success: Concurrent and longitudinal relations', *European Journal of Personality*, 23(2): 71–84.

Tasselli, S., Kilduff, M. & Landis, B. (2018) 'Personality change: Implications for organizational behavior', *The Academy of Management Annals*, 12(2): 467–93.

Tellegen, A. & Waller, N. G. (1987) *Reexamining Basic Dimensions of Natural Language Trait Descriptors*, 95th Annual Meeting of the American Psychological Association, New York.

Tett, R. P., Jackson, D. N. & Rothstein, M. (1991) 'Personality measures as predictors of job performance: A meta-analytic review', *Personnel Psychology*, 44(4): 703–42.

Thomas, J. P., Whitman, D. S. & Viswesvaran, C. (2010) 'Employee proactivity in organizations: A comparative meta-analysis of emergent proactive constructs', *Journal of Occupational and Organizational Psychology*, 83(2): 275–300.

Tornau, K. & Frese, M. (2013) 'Construct clean-up in proactivity research: A meta-analysis on the nomological net of work-related proactivity concepts and their incremental validities', *Applied Psychology: An International Review*, 62(1): 44–96.

Tupes, E. C, & Christal, R. E. (1992) 'Recurrent Personality Factors Based on Trait Ratings', *Journal of Personality*, 60(2): 225–51.

Turnley, W. H. & Feldman, D. C. (1999) 'The impact of psychological contract violations on exit, voice, loyalty, and neglect', *Human Relations*, 52(7): 895–922.

van Vuuren, C. V. & Klandermans, P. G. (1990) 'Individual reactions to job insecurity: An integrated model', in P. J. D. Drenth, J. A. Sergeant & R. J. Takens (eds), *European Perspectives in Psychology* (Vol 3, pp 133–46). Oxford, England: John Wiley & Sons.

Vandewater, E. A. & Stewart, A. J. (1997) 'Women's career commitment patterns and personality development', in M. E. Lachman & J. B. James (eds), *Multiple Paths of Midlife Development* (pp 375–411), Chicago: University of Chicago Press.

Viswesvaran, C. & Ones, D. S. (2010) 'Employee selection in times of change', in G. P. Hodgkinson & J. K. Ford (eds), *International Review of Industrial and Organizational Psychology* (Vol 25, pp 169–226). Chichester: John Wiley & Sons.

Wang, D., Cui, H. & Zhou, F. (2005) 'Measuring the personality of Chinese: QZPS versus NEO PI-R', *Asian Journal of Social Psychology*, 8(1): 97–122.

Wang, Q., Bowling, N. A. & Eschleman, K. J. (2010) 'A meta-analytic examination of work and general locus of control', *Journal of Applied Psychology*, 95(4): 761–8.

Wang, Y., Wu, C. H., Parker, S. K. & Griffin, M. A. (2018) 'Developing goal orientations conducive to learning and performance: An intervention study', *Journal of Occupational and Organizational Psychology*, 91(4): 875–95.

Wille, B. & De Fruyt, F. (2014) 'Vocations as a source of identity: Reciprocal relations between Big Five personality traits and RIASEC characteristics', *Journal of Applied Psychology*, 99: 262–81.

Wille, B., Beyers, W. & De Fruyt, F. (2012) 'A transactional approach to person–environment fit: Reciprocal relations between personality development and career role growth across young to middle adulthood', *Journal of Vocational Behavior*, 81(3): 307–21.

Wille, B., Hofmans, J., Lievens, F., Back, M. D. & De Fruyt, F. (2019) 'Climbing the corporate ladder and within-person changes in narcissism: Reciprocal relationships over two decades', *Journal of Vocational Behavior*, 115, 103341.

Woods, S. A., Lievens, F., De Fruyt, F. & Wille, B. (2013) 'Personality across work life: The longitudinal and reciprocal influences of personality on work', *Journal of Organizational Behavior*, 34(S1): S7–S25.

Woods, S. A., Wille, B., Wu, C. H., Lievens, F., & De Fruyt, F. (2019) 'The influence of work on personality trait development: The demands-affordances TrAnsactional (DATA) model, an integrative review, and research agenda', *Journal of Vocational Behavior*, 110: 258–71.

Woods, S. A., Edmonds, G. W., Hampson, S. E. & Lievens, F. (2020) 'How our work influences who we are: Testing a theory of vocational and personality development over fifty years', *Journal of Research in Personality*, 85, 103930.

Wrzesniewski, A. & Dutton, J. E. (2001) 'Crafting a job: Revisioning employees as active crafters of their work', *Academy of Management Review*, 26(2): 179–201.

Wrzus, C. & Mehl, M. R. (2015) 'Lab and/or Field? Measuring Personality Processes and Their Social Consequences', *European Journal of Personality*, 29(2): 250–71.

Wrzus, C. & Roberts, B. W. (2017) 'Processes of personality development in adulthood: The TESSERA framework', *Personality and Social Psychology Review*, 21(3): 253–77.

Wu, C. H. (2016) 'Personality change via work: A job demand–control model of Big-five personality changes', *Journal of Vocational Behavior*, 92: 157–66.

Wu, C. H. & Griffin, M. A. (2012) 'Longitudinal reciprocal relationships between core self-evaluations and job satisfaction', *Journal of Applied Psychology*, 97(2): 331–42.

Wu, C. H., Griffin, M. A. & Parker, S. K. (2015) 'Developing agency through good work: Longitudinal effects of job autonomy and skill utilization on locus of control', *Journal of Vocational Behavior*, 89: 102–8.

Wu, C. H., Wang, Y., Parker, S. K. & Griffin, M. A. (2020) 'Effects of chronic job insecurity on Big Five personality change', *Journal of Applied Psychology*, 105(11): 1308–26.

Zhang, F. & Parker, S. K. (2019) 'Reorienting job crafting research: A hierarchical structure of job crafting concepts and integrative review', *Journal of Organizational Behavior*, 40(2): 126–46.

Zhang, Z., Wang, M. & Shi, J. (2012), 'Leader-follower congruence in proactive personality and work outcomes: The mediating role of leader–member exchange', *Academy of Management Journal*, 55(1): 111–30.

Zimmermann, J. & Neyer, F. J. (2013) 'Do we become a different person when hitting the road? Personality development of sojourners', *Journal of Personality and Social Psychology*, 105(3): 515–30.

Index

Page numbers in *italics* refer to figures.